Your First Foal

Your First Foal

Horse breeding for beginners

Karin Kattwinkel

Copyright 2005 by Cadmos Verlag, Brunsbek
Typesetting and design: Ravenstein, Verden
Illustations: Maria Mähler
Cover: Christiane Slawik
Printing: Nørhaven, Viborg

Printed in Denmark
ISBN 3-86127-918-5

CONTENTS

Foreword 8

First considerations 10
Stable and environmental requirements 10
What will your foal cost? 13
Selling your foal 14
Assessing your mare as a breeding prospect 14
   Only the best is good enough 14
How to find the right stallion for your mare 15

Some early decisions 18
What do you want your foal to be? 18
Breeding societies and stud books 19
   The international hot blood breeds 19
   Native poy breeds 19
   Other pony stud books 20
   Warmblood and sport horse breeds 20
   Heavy horse breeds 21
   Colour specific breeds 21
   Other horse breeds 21
Checking your foal is eligible for registration 21

A brief introduction to equine genetics 22
Genes 22
Size 23
'Birds and the bees' for horse owners 24
   Male reproductive organs 24

Female reproductive organs 24
The mare's cycle 27
Detecting when the mare is in season 27
Record keeping 28
Veterinary examinations 29
Swabs 29
Vaccinations 29
Other things to remember 31
   Feeding of mare before mating 31

Covering the mare 32
Mating in a herd 32
Teasing 33
Identifying the right moment for covering 34
Artificial insemination or natural mating? 34
Supervised covering 34
Artificial insemination 35
Only for professionals – embryo transfer 36
What costs are involved? 37
Deal with mating injuries 37

A new life develops 38
Fertilisation 38
Has the mating been successful? 39
Development of the foal 39
   Providing for the foetus 40
   Pregnancy testing 40
Fertility problems in the mare 40

The mare is too fat! 40

Misalignment of the vulva 40

Abnormal cycle 40

Oestrus without ovulation.............................40

Late ovulation 41

Ovulation in the middle of the cycle 41

Prolonged intervals between cycles 41

Silent season 41

Aggressive behaviour

during season 41

Possible complications during pregnancy 42

Causes of non-contagious abortions 42

Bacterial infection of the uterus 42

Fever..42

Malnutrition 43

Accidents or exhaustion 43

How to deal with viral abortion...........................43

Twins 44

Caring for the highly pregnant mare..............45

Exercise in every weather 45

Keeping the mare fit...46

Foaling...47

Final preparations 47

Worming 47

The importance of peace and quiet....................48

Signs of impending birth 48

The normal birth...48

Inducing birth..51

The new-born foal...52

Caring for the very young foal 52

Imprinting by the mare.......................................53

Human imprinting 54

Changing behaviour in the mare 55

When something goes wrong 56

The amniotic sack doesn't break 56

The birth process ceases 56

Breached presentation 57

One leg is trapped 57

The foal is too big for the mare..........................57

Torn uterus 58

Retention of the afterbirth...................................58

Damaged vertebrae or pelvis

in the mare...58

Aggressive behaviour of the mare 58

When the first excitement is over 60

Checking that the foal is healthy........................60

Colostrum: the natural vaccine 61

The importance of hygiene 62

Eating droppings in the first few days 63

When to feed extra milk 63

Allergic reaction to colostrum 64

Mastitis...64

Death of the mare...64

Covering the mare again 65

Diseases of the foal 66

Meconium retention..67

Joint-ill 69

Diarrhoea 70

Non contagious intestinal infection

in new-born foals...70

Contagious intestinal infection 70

Physiological diarrhoea (normal) on day 9 70

Infectious arthritis 71

Navel infection 72

Hernia..72

Ruptured bladder 72

Upper airway infection 72

Pneumonia 73

Strangles..73

Correct feeding of the mare and foal..............74

Feeding during pregnancy and lactation............74

The danger of over feeding 75

Increased nutritional needs

in the final stage of pregnancy 76

Feeding following foaling 77

Registering and showing your foal..................79

More on breed society registration 79

Equine passports...80

Preparations for a show.......................................81

Looking right 81

Correct loading of mare and foal 81

Handling the growing foal 82

The importance of companionship 82

The foal's first teeth...84

Worming 84

Vaccinations 85

Providing the essentials.......................................86

Turn out 88

What every foal must learn 88

Foot care 91

Conformational problems 92

Hereditary contracted tendons 93

Club foot..94

Acquired contracted tendons

in the yearling 94

Unequal leg length..94

Additional feeding 95

Extra portions 98

Non- traumatic weaning......................................99

Horses as herd animals.................................100

Some final reminders 103

Freedom of turn out 104

Important facts about postures 105

The factors that influence growth 106

The arrival of sexual maturity 107

Growth rates..107

How to recognise the foal's future potential 109

Useful addresses 111

FOREWORD

Seeing your own foal develop from an embryo into a promising youngster is one of the most rewarding experiences a horse lover can encounter. In this book, I aim to explain what you need to know in order for you to enjoy your foal to the full. Even if some of the subjects I cover might seem a little off-putting, my intention is always to give you the information you need that will not only help you to make an informed decision but also help you to recognise potential problem areas and hopefully prevent them before they arise. This approach will benefit both your beloved mare and the foal you plan to have from her and your own enjoyment of them.

But first you need to be really honest with yourself and ask: 'Is my favourite mare actually suitable to be bred from?' Only if you are absolutely sure that the answer is 'yes' should you proceed any further with your breeding plans.

Far too often, worn out or unrideable mares are used for breeding, based on the argument 'if I cannot ride her any more she should at least have a foal'. As many problems are hereditary, this is not an ideal way to select breeding stock, because progeny of such parents often have the same problems as their sires and dams. This is why the idea that breeding a foal from your own mare means that you can get a new horse or pony cheaply is often a false one. Breeding from a mare and raising its foal, delightful activities as they are, requires a lot of care, patience and knowledge as well as money and time. Being able to cope with problems – because set-backs and disappointments are part of every breeder's life – and the support of your family or your partner are therefore essential.

You should also remember that mistakes made in the foal's first few months will influence its whole life. It will be a good four years before the foal can be ridden, and in no other species is managing the growing phase as important as it is in the horse. This is because the early days determine the development of the skeleton and constitution and therefore its suitability for performance or pleasure. Incorrect management as a foal can finish a promising career prematurely. The temperament of the youngster may also suffer if it is not raised in a horse-specific environment including sufficient space in the stable and field and equine companions of the same age. Keeping a mare and foal on their own behind the house has nothing to do with animal welfare, it is pure egoism.

Affection, reason and careful attention to detail are other important requirements for a breeder. You should be a guide for your young animal. Only then can you shape its character and ensure that it is well-mannered and has a good temperament. Far too often, however, people do not treat their horses consistently. In successful human-equine relations, the human being has to be the leader from the start and needs to be shown respect at all times without compromise. The equine should always be an inferior herd member, a role that suits a herd animal well as it provides security and protection.

Last but not least you should be able to recognise your own limits and ask for competent help and advice when necessary.

Enjoy this book and I hope that it helps you breed a foal that is all you wanted,

Karin Kattwinkel

An open-sided barn or field shelter with access to grass and other mares and foals for company is a good environment for mares and foals as it can be adjusted to their changing needs.
Photo: Chr. Slawik

FIRST CONSIDERATIONS

Stable and environmental requirements

Conventional stable yards, particularly those designed for riding horses are not really suitable for brood mares and foals. This is because, in the last third of pregnancy, the mare needs a quieter environment and an undisturbed retreat. She should also not be exposed to new horses on a regular basis as there is a risk of in-fection from them. For the actual birth, she needs a clean separate area with plenty of straw somewhere that the foaling can easily be observed. Even native breeds may require assistance and a muddy shared paddock is not suitable.

Foaling outside is ideal for hygienic reasons

but it is difficult to observe. Mares, particularly maidens with a first foal, fiercely protect their newborn from other horses and people. A spacious stable gives them the necessary peace and quiet during this important bonding phase. However, locking up a mare used to living in a herd in a stable without visual contact with other horses is not a good idea. It causes far too much stress!

If you cannot offer your mare a suitable area for foaling and for the first few weeks after the birth, it is better to take her to an experienced breeder to foal down. Your foal will then also have playmates to grow up with. Understandably, every owner would like to see their 'once in a lifetime' foal being born and grow up and have it all to themselves. The welfare of mother and foal, however, should always be more important than the fulfilment of your own dreams. If you really do not wish to send the mare away for foaling a possible compromise is to alter your stable lay out to suit her needs. Perhaps you could do it together with another local single-mare-owning breeder? Whatever arrangement you choose, the most important requirement is a large, high-quality pasture. A young foal should be turned out during summer, day and night! For this reason alone, most riding stables are not ideal for breeding.

Advice
Make sure there are no hazards in the vicinity of the mare and foal. No protruding nails, sharp edges, small gaps (under doors and partitions as well), no hayracks in which the small feet of a foal could get trapped.

The most important questions for new breeders are:

- **What do you want your foal to become?**
Do you want an eventer, show jumper, dressage star, hunter, show pony, endurance horse or an all-round pleasure horse for the family? Set a specific goal and choose the sire and dam accordingly.

- **Are you going to keep your foal or sell it?**
Do you want to ride your youngster yourself? Can you break it in yourself? Do you want to sell it as a weanling, a just-backed youngster or as an educated adult horse?

- **Do you have sufficient space to raise a foal and possibly keep it for 4 years or even the rest of its life?**
Is the stable and pasture suitable for a brood mare and her youngster?

- **Have you got enough time to look after them properly?**
A mare and foal need as much time as a riding horse, possibly even more!

- **Is your knowledge of how to handle and raise a foal sufficient to deal with all situations**

- **Do you know enough about breeding?**
Or are you at least prepared to learn everything you need?

- **Are you persistent enough?**
Horse breeding requires persistence. Success takes time, setbacks are common. It takes years before your dream of an adult horse becomes true.

- **Do you have enough money?**
Attempting to breed your own foal can be very expensive. It is not a way to get a cheap replacement for your mare. Keep savings for additional vet's bills and extras.

- **What does your family say about it?**
Not an unimportant question, especially if they are not as enthusiastic as you are.

What will your foal cost you?

Because the ever-rising costs of everything from hay to vaccinations vary from area to area, and because the needs of a native pony broodmare and her foal are somewhat different to those of a thin-coated Thoroughbred or a finely-tuned warmblood, it is impossible to give an exact figure in answer to this question. However, you must know your own accurate costings before you make the decision about whether or not to breed from your mare, so use the checklist below to help you compile the relevant costs.

Up until the time of weaning, you have to expect the following costs:

Insurance for mare and foal
Feed
- Hard feed, 1 ton
- Hay, 1 ton
- Straw, 2 tons
- Food supplements, 50 kg

Pasture (fencing, fertiliser)
Covering (stud fee)
Transport
Electricity, water
Farrier for mare and foal
Breeding society membership and registration fees
Veterinary costs
- Swab
- Follicle check and ultrasound
- Pregnancy test
- Vaccinations
- Neugeborenenuntersuchung
- Worming mare and foal
- Contigency fund for veterinary costs

Contingency fund for other additional costs

Professional breeders also have to consider:
Value of the mare
10 years of use
Rates
Staff salaries and National Insurance contributions
Maintenance of buildings
Employers and third-party public insurance

Unexpected costs like illness or injury can increase the total significantly.

Successful breeding has to involve selection – choosing the best animals for your breeding programme and disregarding the bad ones! Photo: K. Kattwinkel

Selling your foal

If you want to sell your foal you should chose the mare and stallion especially carefully. A foal that fulfils your expectations regarding looks and conformation can usually be sold just through word of mouth. Other options are advertisements on the internet or in dedicated magazines and specialist selected auctions are also an increasingly popular choice. Your breed society (which is almost certainly listed in the addresses section at the end of the book) can usually give you information about these.

Assessing your mare as a breeding prospect

Only the best is good enough
Try to be as objective as possible when deciding whether your mare is really suited to becoming a mother. You and your possible buyer will certainly enjoy owning a sound, talented and trainable animal much more than one that

is unsound, unrideable or unmanageable as a result of a poor breeding decision.

The potential broodmare should have a friendly personality and should not display vices like weaving, crib biting, or kicking. This is not only important because these vices could be hereditary, but also because the mare would be a bad example to her foal if she showed them. There is also always the risk that the mare could hurt her foal if she became very ill-tempered in its presence.

It goes without saying that the mare should be physically healthy. If your mare can no longer be ridden for health reasons (e. g. it is lame or has a chronic cough) you must consult your vet first to find out if these problems might be hereditary. If they are, you should abandon the idea of breeding from her.

If a mare has had to retire due to misman-agement or injury that is not the result of a conformational defect (e. g. a non-hereditary problem, the vet should establish if pregnancy and birth would be too demanding for her. If the mare has already had a foal when younger, using her again for breeding at a later stage is certainly an option. She should, however, not be older than 16 years when having her first foal.

In order to establish her sexual health, you can examine the mare's udder and her genital area initially yourself. The udder should be symmetrical and have two equally sized teats. Check the position of her vulva (indication of possible problems with the uterus) and its alignment (a gap increases the risk of infection). However, the examination of the internal organs has to be carried out by a vet (the first of many costs that you will encounter). Immature mares often give birth to small and weak foals.

Also, young mares may not have had time to develop properly themselves and their immature bones will be under a lot of stress from the weight of the foal including the placenta and also from insufficient calcification, as the growing foal is given a higher priority. Unfortunately, these processes cannot be compensated for even by optimal mineral supply in the feed and the consequences only show up later in life when the mare is being ridden and then shows early signs of wear and tear. You should therefore not cover your mare before she is three years old. Breeds that mature late should really be given another year before being put in foal and some stud books – especially those of the native pony breeds – refuse to register foals born to mares below a certain age to ensure that this happens. On the other hand, experienced sport horse breeders

50 per cent of a foal's genes, but 60 per cent of its behaviour, come from the mother. A brood mare should therefore have an outstanding temperament. Photo: N. Sachs

sometimes cover very tall mares at the age of two years old, as the pregnancy will usually stop their excessive growth.

How to find the right stallion for your mare

When choosing the future sire of your foal you should consider the following:
1. Do not just choose the stallion because you

Check out the future father yourself. Photos can be mislead-ing! Check his behaviour, as he passes on not only his appear-ance but also his character. You also need to check that he is approved for breeding by an appropriate breed society as oth-erwise his foals will not be eligible for pedigree papers and thus worth less. Photo: Chr. Slawik

like him but visualise how you want your new foal to look at maturity and what purpose it should fulfil. Is he suitable for your mare or are both so fundamentally different that the result could be a mismatch?

2. Compare the pedigree of the stallion with that of your mare. Although some world class show jumpers and dressage horses appear to be quite closely line-bred, this is a very skilled operation and not for the amateur breeder. In general, therefore, mutual ancestors should not appear earlier than the third generation.

3. The stallion should have his strengths where the mare has her weaknesses. It is by no means always the case that the foal will then be an equal mixture of mother's and father's influ-ences but the possibility is higher in a case where the stallion has the same weakness as the mare.

4. Observe the stallion's character and tempera-

ment as well. Choose a calm and relaxed stallion for a nervous mare. You should never consider a stallion with a difficult character or vices.

If at all possible, go and see the stallion your-self. Only then can you form an opinion as to his conformation, temperament, charisma, be-haviour and ridability. If he is too far away ask at least for some video footage. It is also rec-ommended to check out some of his offspring.

Some pre-potent stallions pass on their char-acteristics strongly, even when using very dif-ferent mares. Others produce foals that always look like their mothers. Some have a good mix-ture of foals. By looking at his foals, you can gather important information about this, which will help you to decide which stallion to choose

When choosing the sire of your foal you need to know how prepotent he is. In other words, does he pass on his characteristics strongly or do his foals usually look like their mother? Photo: S. Schomburg

if you want to correct small faults in your mare or if you want a close image of her.

Choosing a stallion with an elegant, small head can compensate one single fault, for example a heavy head of the mare. Many faults, however, cannot be balanced out by choosing a suitable sire. A successful breeder will therefore always prefer a horse with one big fault but many good points, rather than a horse with lots of small faults. Such judgements should be left in the hands of the experts. They require a lot of experience and the right intuition.

When visiting the future sire, use the opportunity to check out the stud. Are high standards of care and good hygiene for your mare guaranteed? Do not hesitate to ask questions and check out the mare's stable, covering area and paddocks. A responsible stud manager will understand your concern. For that reason alone, a visit to the stud is worthwhile: at least you will not turn up with your mare on the trailer and ask yourself whether you should turn around and leave straight away!

If your mare is registered with a breed society and you also want your foal to be registered you need to choose a stallion that is approved for breeding with them. The breeding society in question can advise you where to find a stallion. A growing number of studs also hold the British Equestrian Federation (BEF) British Breeder's Quality Mark award which ensures that the stud is run to a high standard of safety for your mare and her foal. Details of these studs are available from the Breeding section of the BEF at www.bef.co.uk/britishbreeding.htm

Photo: N. Sachs

SOME EARLY DECISIONS

What do you want your foal to be?

Even if you have no intention of selling your youngster it is sensible to have proper papers for it and equine passports are now compul-

sory throughout the European Union. You cannot know how your circumstances may change in the future and you may be forced to sell your foal, in which case pedigree papers and a passport will be essential. More positively, perhaps you want to affiliate it in order to compete, but in either case you can only apply for pedigree papers for offspring from registered parents approved for breeding.

Breed societies and stud books

There are well over 40 different breed societies in the UK and all of them have different requirements for registration. Of these at least 10, chiefly Moorland and Mountain breeds such as the Exmoor Pony Society and the Shetland Pony Stud-Book Society, are mother stud books and are vital sources of long-term breed histories. Mother stud books are recognised as the foundation stud books of the breed and all other recognised stud books for the breed elsewhere in the world are termed daughter stud books and must follow the breed standards and registration procedures laid down by the mother stud book as closely as possible within the legal framework of the relevant national breeding laws.

Stud books in the UK generally fall into one of the following groups listed below.

The international hot blood breeds

There are two major pure-bred hot blood 'light horse' stud books in the world, namely the Thoroughbred (registered in the General Stud Book maintained by Wetherbys) and the Arab (the pedigree records of which are kept by the Arab Horse Society).

Unique amongst stud books in the UK, the General Stud Book, which is primarily designed for race horses, requires no licensing or veterinary inspections for its stallions or mares. It is the international arbiter of Thoroughbred pedigrees in the world and all other Thoroughbred breeding organisations (such as the French and American Jockey Clubs) are subject to its rulings. Pedigree authentification is done by a combination of covering returns, identity diagram and DNA testing and no further qualification is required as pedigree records go back undiluted by unproven crosses for over 250 years. However, there is also a part-bred section, known as Wetherbys Non-Thoroughbred Register. This is open to non-Thoroughbred mares that have been covered by Thoroughbred stallions, to non-Thoroughbred stallions that have successfully passed a thorough vetting inspection and also – in due course – to the parentage-tested offspring of these stallions and mares. Many top class eventers have what are known as NTR papers as a high percentage of Thoroughbred blood is considered desirable for this sport,

The Arab Horse Society was the first stud book for pure-bred Arab horses in the world. It is also a founder member of the World Arab Horse Organisation (WAHO) and its pedigree papers (which are DNA-tested for parentage verification) are therefore recognised world wide. Licensing of stallions is by veterinary inspection, although there is also an optional Premium performance scheme for competing stallions. There are also thriving Anglo Arab and part-bred Arab registers, which ensure that a considerable number of competition animals are also registered in them.

Native pony breeds

There are 11 native pony breeds unique to the UK and they are often referred to as the glory of the British horse world. These breeds (Dales, Dartmoors, Exmoors, Fells, Highlands, New Forests, and four different breeds of Welsh) all have very strict policies on stallion licensing and approval to ensure that the bloodlines and true native type of the breed are preserved. Only progeny of fully licensed stallions out of mares also fully registered in the stud book are eligible for pure-bred papers (now in the form of an equine passport with a verified pedigree) and some breeds such as the Exmoor will only provide these to pure-bred foals after they have been individually inspected and approved according to the physical requirements of the breed standard. Numbers registered each year vary widely amongst the stud books with some (Dartmoor, Exmoor etc) being officially recognised as Rare Breeds, whilst others have extensive part-bred stud books for animals by or out of one fully registered parent which helps to swell the numbers. The native pony breeds of the UK are not only unique but they also have outstanding qualities of soundness and good temperament and as a result many have also developed a strong following overseas where many daughter stud books exist for specific breeds.

Other pony stud books

These include more general pony stud books such as the National Pony Society and the Sports Pony Studbook Society, plus those (usually daughter) organisations that register foreign pony breeds such as the Caspian, Icelandic and Norwegian Fjord. All licence stallions with some form of inspection and some (such as the Sports Pony Studbook Society) also insist on inspections for mares wishing to enter the stud book,

Warmblood and sport horse breeds

There are currently about a dozen of these operating in the UK and all have comprehensive systems of inspection, licensing and approval (grading) of stallions and mares based upon conformation, paces, performance (own and progeny's), pedigree and veterinary inspection in line with the standard procedures encouraged by the World Breeding Federation for Sport Horses (WBFSH). Four of the breeds are home grown, namely the Anglo-European Studbook (AES), the British Warm-Blood Society (BWBS), the Scottish Sports Horse (SSH) and Sport Horse Breeding Society of Great Britain (SHBGB), originally the Hunters Improvement Society, then the National Light Horse Breeding Society before it became IDHS (GB) in 1999; all of these organisations inspect and approve across a wide range of sport horse and warm blood breeds destined for competition in the three Olympic disciplines of dressage, eventing and show jumping although in general the BWBS is best known for dressage, SHGB for eventing and the AES and SSH for show jumping. The remaining stud books are daughter stud books of foreign breed societies and usually follow the grading and registration rules of their mother societies to the letter – the British Hannoverian Horse Society (BHHS) is a prime example of this – although some (such as the Irish Draught Horse Society of Great Britain (ISHGB) have increased the importance of their part-bred (sport horse) sections to reflect the interests of British breeders. Interestingly, the Cleveland Bay (sometimes erroneously described as the original warmblood breed of Britain) was once bred solely as a carriage horse but despite the popularity of driving is now the only UK riding horse breed that is also a Rare Breed. However, it is popular as a source of show jumping blood and the part-bred Cleveland Bay (usually a Thoroughbred X CB) is often to be seen performing at the highest levels in this sport. The increasingly rare Hackney horse is also in this category.

Heavy horse breeds

Three of these – Clydesdale, Shire and Suffolk – are British breeds, with the Suffolk sadly being classified as a Rare Breed. The other is the Percheron, originally a French breed but well-established here for very many years. Again all stallions are licensed but no part-bred stock are registered, only pure-breds. When an outcross does take place, it is generally in the form of covering a heavy horse mare with a Thoroughbred stallion and the resulting progeny are then generally eligible for registration with either Wetherbys NTR or SHBGB (or often both)!

Colour-specific breeds

Some of these are imported breeds with long-established pedigree records (e. g. the Appaloosa) whilst others are entirely colour-based (e. g. the Coloured Horse and Pony Society or CHAPS). All of them inspect for correct colour and markings as well as veterinary soundness and will only provide stud book pedigree papers for progeny of approved bloodlines that are correctly marked. However, in general, these stud books will also issue pedigree papers and passports to solid-coloured offspring of graded, correctly coloured parents although they will not approve such animals for breed-

ing purposes even though they approve correctly marked/coloured animals of unknown breeding for breeding purposes.

Other horse breeds

This group is mainly made up of imported breeds that appeal to specific interest groups such as American Quarter Horses (Reining), Lippizaners (classical dressage) and the spectacular Andalusians, Lusitanos and Morgan Horses, who all have stringent stallion licensing procedures, enthusiastic supporters and thriving part-bred stud books.

Checking your foal is eligible for registration

Whichever stallion you choose, and whatever stud book you choose to register your foal with, you must check that the stallion's progeny are eligible for that stud book, that the covering certificate you will be given once your mare is mated is acceptable to the stud book and that the stallion owner will be including your mare on his list of mares covered that is submitted to that stud book. If any of these requirements are not in order when you come to register your foal expensive problems may arise, particularly if your mare has been approved by another stud book. With many stallions and mares being accepted by several stud books at different levels, mistakes can – and do – occur so you need to check this very carefully.

You can safely assume that everything can be inherited from markings to behaviour - that also applies to the less likable characteristics of your mare. Photo: N. Sachs

A BRIEF INTRODUCTION TO EQUINE GENETICS

Genes

The inherited characteristics of a horse not only depend on both parents, but also to a lesser degree on grand- and great-grandparents and can reach as far back as the fourth (sometimes even sixth) generation. This is the same for horses as it is for humans and applies to mares as well as stallions. Therefore, a parent's own performance is of no more than 20 per cent importance.

Always look at the pedigree of the parents. This is difficult if the horses' ancestors are not known and this will be a risk factor. It is therefore all the more important to choose a stallion that is of similar type and size as the mare

Unfortunately, there is no definite rule that parents of a certain height will produce a foal of the same height.
Photo: S. Schomburg

but has an even better conformation and whose performance is above that of your mare.

A long-established motto in horse breeding is: 'Pair like with like!'. In other words, make sure that the sire and dam are not vastly different. For example, you should not attempt an experiment such as crossing a Hackney Horse with a Suffolk or similar. You rarely get a useful riding horse out of such a pair.

Even a superb mare can sometimes produce a foal that will not match your expectations. The dam may have been a lucky accident of faulty parents or 'does not have a consolidated pedigree' as the experts say. A foal from such a parent will have genes that do not match the high quality of its dam. That is why the practice of breeding specific bloodlines is now so popular. It means that the desired characteristics of an animal are present over many generations. The genes are therefore fairly secure. For example if the direct ancestors of a mare were all excellent show jumpers then this

characteristic has been passed on from animal to animal. Consequently, the probability is also very high that the mare will also pass on this talent.

Size

When pairing a pony mare measuring 12 hh with a stallion measuring 14 hh the foal will not necessarily be 13 hh. This can happen but it is not always the case. Some breeders believe that the stallion determines the size and frame of the foal; whilst others believe it is the mare that does this. You need a lot of experience to make the right decision about this.

In fact, a pony breeder who wants a slightly taller foal might well achieve it better by using a small Arab or Thoroughbred stallion than a big pony stallion. There is no risk that the foal will be too big for the mare because the embryo usually develops in relation to the available space.

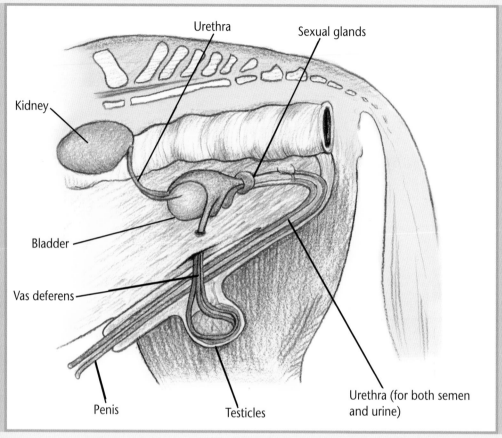

Urethra

Sexual glands

Kidney

Bladder

Vas deferens

Penis

Testicles

Urethra (for both semen and urine)

'Birds and the bees' for horse owners

Male reproductive organs

The testicles and the penis are visible on the outside. Both vas deferens lead to the urethra. The penis has one orifice for both urine and ejaculation. The latter consists of sperm and semen plasma, (which is the transport medium for the journey to the oviduct).

An adult stallion ejaculates between 40 and 80 millilitres of semen and this will contain between 2 and 8 million sperm.

Female reproductive organs

The reproductive organs of the mare are the ovaries and the genital tract formed by oviduct, uterus, cervix, vagina and vulva. The sexual hormones responsible for the cycle are produced by the ovaries, inside the uterus and in the hypothalamus in the brain.

Reproductive organs of the mare

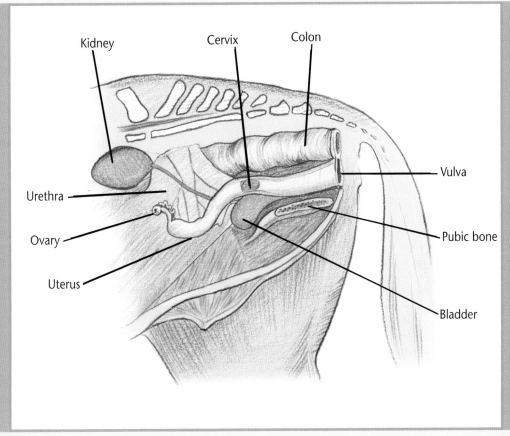

Kidney Cervix Colon

Urethra

Ovary

Uterus

Vulva

Pubic bone

Bladder

A mare is born with many thousands of egg cells in her ovaries. Upon reaching sexual maturity, a follicle develops around the egg cell and this increases in size when she is in season. This follicle produces the hormone oestrogen. During ovulation, the follicle tears and the egg travels through a groove to the oviduct. The inside of the follicle bleeds and a blood clot forms at the point at which the egg was attached. So-called lutein cells, special cells of the follicle membrane, grow into the blood clot and form the corpus luteum. This tissue produces the hormone progesterone (also called the pregnancy hormone). The corpus luteum is active between two cycles (during dioestrus).

The oviduct connects the ovaries and the uterus and opens directly into the uterus at the tips of the uterus horns. The oviduct is where fertilisation takes place when the egg cell travels down the tube after ovulation, the sperm actively moves through the uterus into the oviduct, and both then meet.

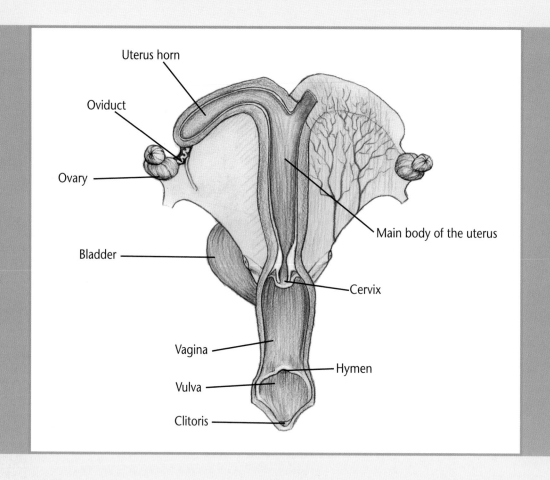

Uterus horn

Oviduct

Ovary

Bladder

Main body of the uterus

Cervix

Vagina

Hymen

Vulva

Clitoris

The fertilised egg then travels to the uterus. Unfertilised eggs, on the other hand are re-absorbed by the mare's body.

The uterus consists of the main body and two horns.

The uterus is lined by a mucus membrane (endometrium) and is fixed to the upper abdominal cavity by a broad ligament, which contains arteries, veins and nerves. During a difficult birth the arteries can tear and if this happens it can often lead to a life-threatening haemorrhage. The main body of the uterus narrows at the end and forms the cervix, part of which protrudes into the vagina. The urethras open into the vagina.

On the outside, the folds of the vulva protect the entrance to the vagina. The vulva contains many sweat and oil glands. A subcutaneous muscle surrounds the clitoris and extends upwards to the anus.

This and another muscle is responsible for the 'flashing' action (the opening and closing of the vulva showing the clitoris), which in many mares is an indication that they are in season.

The mare's cycle

The mare's receptive phase is called her season or oestrus. The mare is in season every 21 days and it lasts about seven to nine days. The cycle often ceases in the autumn and winter. During warm periods, the oestrus can be shorter, often only five days in length. The intensity of the oestrus varies from mare to mare and depends not only on her individual physiology, but also on climate, nutrition and environment. The ovaries are usually inactive during the winter, during which time no follicles or corpora lutea are produced. This phase is called anoestrus.

Whether or not a mare is ready for mating depends on the time of the year. When the days get longer in the spring, the hypothalamus is stimulated and produces sexual hormones, and oestrus symptoms become more obvious. The number of productive egg cells is highest in May, June and July. This is a wise plan of nature: a mare covered during this time will foal in April or May of the following year when it is already warm enough for the foal to survive outside. Sufficient fresh grass also guarantees high quality milk at this time. A foal born in April or May therefore arrives at the best time for a good start in life. Covering a mare earlier in the year may be of economical advantage but it is not the best for her or her foal.

Detecting when the mare is in season

When oestrus is imminent, many mares become increasingly restless or ticklish. During the season, the vulva appears swollen and enlarged. Discharge from the vagina can be seen which in healthy mares should be transparent and clear. The mucus membranes show a red colour. Mares in season urinate more frequently and flick open the vulva repeatedly. If a mare is lactating when in season, their foals often show light diarrhoea for a few days.

'Flashing' is a classic sign of oestrus.
Photo: Chr. Slawik

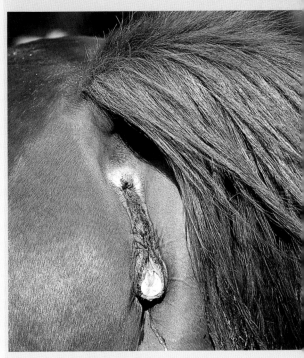

The mare accepts a stallion only during oestrus. To indicate that she is ready to do this she will position her hind legs further apart, lift her tail and discharge a yellow liquid of characteristic smell. (Some mares also show a flehmen expression on their muzzles and nostrils). Finally, the mare accepts the covering.

Between seasons, however, the mare will fight off the stallion by displaying aggression, biting or kicking. At this time she will also hold down her tail or swish it from side to side.

Ovulation takes place halfway between two seasons, although the timing can differ significantly. Some mares ovulate early in the cycle and some towards the end. Nowadays it is common to consult the vet to establish the exact time of ovulation. The vet carries out a manual internal examination of the ovaries and can so determine the progress of the follicle. In order to be absolutely sure, an increasing number of vets also perform an ultrasonic examination (scan) as visual proof of ovulation.

Record keeping

Note on a calendar when your mare is in season. Start this early in the year several cycles before you plan to mate her. You will then get to know the signs of the oestrus she shows and may save yourself many wasted journeys to the stud or insemination centre. You should write down the first and last day of the season and also days with particularly strong signs. You can mark the intensity as follows:

(+) light season: mare wants to be with other horses (especially males), grunts when touched, lifts the tail

(++) moderate season: lifting the tail, flashing

(+++) strong season: mare positions herself with hind legs apart, lifts the tail, flashes und urinates frequently, accepts touching usually without grunting

Important note:
Only when the mare has contact with other horses will you be able to recognise the signs properly.

It is also important to keep a calendar in order to determine the right time for a veterinary examination as rectal examination of ovaries and uterus as well as bacteriological swabs only deliver good results when carried out during oestrus.

If you are unable to detect clear signs of oestrus in your mare ask your vet to examine her ovaries and uterus. Alternatively, if the mare is healthy and all her swabs are clean and her vaccinations up-to-date, take her to the stud. You need to do this because the oestrus signs usually become stronger in the presence of a stallion. An experienced stud manager may also be able to determine the right time for mating even without the mare displaying good signs of oestrus.

With age, the signs of oestrus can become weaker and the cycle may no longer be regular.

In the period between two seasons (dioestrus), the uterus prepares itself for the development of the fertilised egg. The mucus membrane becomes sticky and dry, ready to implant the egg. The egg arrives in the uterus about five to six days after fertilisation.

If it is not fertilised the preparation process will stop at around day 15 in order to allow a new cycle to start.

Veterinary examinations

The vet examines the position, size and thickness of the uterus as well as the size of the ovaries and size and number of follicles either manually or with ultrasound. Make a note whether the ripening follicle is on the left or right side. Usually, the left and right ovaries ovulate alternately.

Some mares grow a smaller (but also ripening) follicle on the other ovary after about 10 days that can induce a weaker oestrus. Such an oestrus is not usually used for mating, as there is a risk of a twin pregnancy.

Using a speculum, the vet can visually examine the cervix and vagina. This examination helps to determine the phase of the cycle and optimal time for covering as well as an existing pregnancy.

Swabs

Most studs require a bacteriological examination (swab) of the mare in order to protect the stallion from sexually transmittable diseases. This examination is also important for the mare: if she is not healthy she is unlikely to become pregnant. The vet will take a swab from the cervix and (for natural mating) from the clitoris using a long, sterile cotton swab which is then examined for bacteria in a laboratory. Ideally, the swab is taken during oestrus as the results will be better and the actual procedure less uncomfortable for the mare.

If the result is negative all is well. In case of a 'positive' result, pathogenic bacteria or fungi will have been found. Treatment of the mare according to the resistance test from the laboratory will then be necessary. The resistance test determines the sensitivity of the infectious agent against certain drugs so that the vet knows exactly which treatment to use. The drugs will either be given by injection or directly into the uterus. Another swab needs to be taken after 21 days to establish whether the treatment was successful. It can take several cycles to clear an infection, which is why an early start is essential. However, remember that a bacteriological examination only makes sense when carried out close to the time of covering. A swab taken in February does not tell you much about the genital health in May.

Vaccinations

Current vaccinations for tetanus, equine influenza, equine herpes and equine viral aerteritis (EVA) may be required if the vet is to visit at stud and your breeding schedule should allow for this.

Mares pass on immunity to their foal via their milk. The youngster is protected until it is old enough to be vaccinated itself. Newborn foals can easily pick up a tetanus infection through the navel. Tetanus bacteria are everywhere in

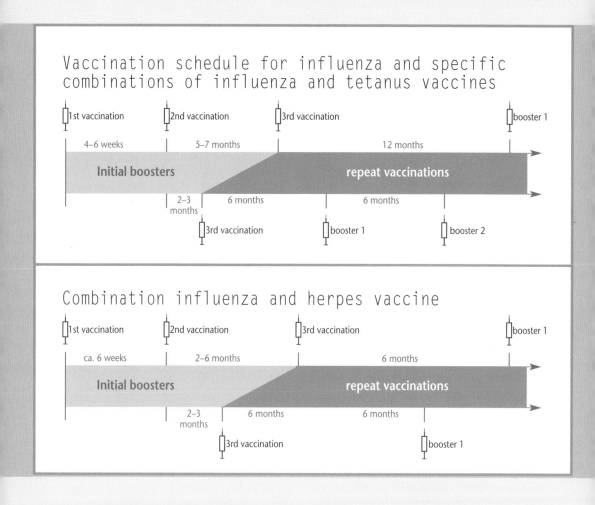

Vaccination schedule for influenza and specific combinations of influenza and tetanus vaccines

1st vaccination   2nd vaccination   3rd vaccination   booster 1

4–6 weeks   5–7 months   12 months

Initial boosters   **repeat vaccinations**

2–3 months   6 months   6 months

3rd vaccination   booster 1   booster 2

Combination influenza and herpes vaccine

1st vaccination   2nd vaccination   3rd vaccination   booster 1

ca. 6 weeks   2–6 months   6 months

Initial boosters   **repeat vaccinations**

2–3 months   6 months   6 months

3rd vaccination   booster 1

a stable, no matter how hygienic it is. Chances of recovery from a tetanus infection are, even with the most intensive treatment, as good as nil. Preventative vaccination is therefore essential.

The mare should also be vaccinated against viral abortion. There are various vaccines available that offer sufficient protection and it is best to consult your vet on this. Mares that are properly vaccinated against herpes virus and whose vaccinations have not lapsed are pro-

tected anyway, provided the boosters are administered regularly during pregnancy as well. If your mare has not already been vaccinated against the herpes virus she will then need to have boosters in months 3 or 4 and again at months 7 or 8 of her pregnancy.

You should also bear in mind that it is sensible to vaccinate all your horses against herpes to ensure all round maximum protection.

Other things to remember

A special worming before covering is not necessary provided the mare has been wormed regularly. Some studs may require proof of worming by a vet to protect their own livestock (ask beforehand) but, worming a month or two before mating is recommended so that the mare does not need to be wormed during the first three months of pregnancy (the most sensitive phase).

Regular foot care is of course important, because the mare has to carry not only her own weight but also that of the foal. Pregnant women often notice how uncomfortable badly fitting shoes are during that time and the same is true for broodmares when their shoes are badly fitted, the time between farriers appointments increases or their feet are not trimmed and become too long.

Feeding the mare before mating

Towards the end of winter, the vitamin A content of all stored feeds decreases (e. g. hay loos-es about 10 per cent per month). As vitamin A is so important for fertility, it is recommended that a warmblood brood mare is fed about 3 kg a day) and receives a vitamin supplement with plenty of vitamin E, B and trace elements and minerals plus 2–3 kgs of high quality lucerne hay. If you cannot buy lucerne hay you can replace it with 1–2 kgs of a special concentrate especially for brood mares that has a higher protein content (14 to 16 per cent) and contains beta carotin. Do not forget to adjust other concentrates accordingly. With this mixture, you imitate spring food and the mare's cycle will improve. This will increase fertility especially in older mares.

Thoroughbred mares should be allowed to follow a similar feeding schedule, but it may be increased or decreased according to the amount of condition (fat and muscle) they are carrying.

Pony mares are unlikely to require so much extra feed because they are much better food converters (good doers), especially the native breeds. Even so, they do still require additional vitamins and minerals to ensure the correct development of the embryo.

During natural mating foal will stand in front of the mare.
Photo: Chr. Slawik

COVERING
THE MARE

Due to human interference, only a few horses can display natural sexual behaviour. Usually, a totally unnatural behaviour is forced upon them.

Under natural conditions, a stallion lives with a herd of mares and sexual behaviour induces no aggression from either party. The stallion approaches the mare only when he can detect sign of oestrus, otherwise he leaves her in peace. Therefore there is no reason for the mare to fend the stallion off as she may need to do under more controlled conditions in a confined space.

Mating in a herd

Native breeds are usually still allowed to breed naturally. The stallion lives with his mares either all year round or only during the breeding season. Studs that allow stallions to run with their mares but also have visiting mares often practise a rotational system so that the mare develops naturally. The stallion is then introduced to these mare herds in turn.

Fertility rates for natural mating in a herd are much higher (over 90 per cent) compared to artificial insemination (sometimes as low as 50 per cent if insemination does not take place at the optimum time).

Teasing

For teasing, the mare is presented to the stallion, safely protected by a strong wall, with her head first. If the mare accepts the contact on

The solid wall of the teasing stocks protects the stallion if the mare tries to fend him off. Photo: Maierhofer

Mating in a herd

Advantages
- *Species-specific environment*
- *Continuous exercise*
- *Natural hierarchy in the herd*
- *Hardly any aggression between mare and stallion*
- *High fertility rate (over 90 per cent)*

Disadvantages
- *Higher risk of injury (mainly as a result of fighting between unfamiliar mares)*
- *No chance of interference in case of problems during mating*
- *Only practical for stallions not in high demand*
- *Mares stay at studs for longer*
- *Long journeys may be necessary*
- *Mare and stallion cannot be used for any other purpose during the breeding season*

head and neck she is then encouraged to stand parallel to the wall so that the stallion can extend his contact along the whole body to the rump. Some mares are at first aggressive and unfriendly but this should stop after a while if she is in season and ready to be mated.

It is therefore important to allow sufficient time for mare and stallion to get to know each other. We must not forget that this type of initial contact is very unnatural for horses.

At many commercial studs a 'teaser' stallion is used, whose sole responsibility is testing the mares. The covering stallion is only taken to the mare once the teasing stallion has established that the mare is ready for mating. This will be when the mare has shown interest in the teaser stallion, positioning her hind legs, flashing and producing mucous urine. A teasing stallion may also used when carrying out artificial insemination.

Identifying the right moment for covering

The mare should be covered between 6 and 24 hours before ovulation to ensure that a sufficient number of mature sperm are in the oviduct just before ovulation. Although only one single sperm fertilises the egg, it seems to be important to have a high number of them present. It has been suggested that all the sperm together produce certain enzymes that are vital for the penetration into the egg cell. The egg cell can be fertilised for about 24 hours.

A second mating is usually carried out 48 hours after the first one.

Artificial insemination or natural mating?

Unless you decide to purchase fresh transported, chilled or frozen semen from a specific stallion, the choice of whether you use artificial insemination or have your mare naturally covered is often not yours but is decided by the stud depending on which stallion you want to use. For health and management reasons, stallions that are used for artificial insemination are unlikely to be used also for natural covering and vice versa, so you need to bear this in mind when looking for a stallion.

When using natural mating, you usually need to leave your mare at the stud for a few days. Specialist insemination centres can be the exception however, and you may be able to take your mare home again straight after a successful covering. Even so, you may have to travel there again for a pregnancy scan or for a second insemination if the mare does not conceive after the first covering.

Supervised covering

The top of the tail is usually bandaged, the genital and anal area thoroughly washed and disinfected and soft pads (kicking boots) put on the hind feet. Sometimes the mare will be twitched, a front leg is held up or her hind legs tied. Even if this is difficult for you to accept, you have little choice as the owner of the mare because these procedures are done for the safety of the stallion.

Discuss the procedure of covering with the stud manager so that you are prepared and can prevent your mare getting frightened. It is advisable to wear hats and have the mare wearing kicking boots. Photo: Chr. Slawik

Supervised covering

Advantages
- *Difficult stallions can be better controlled*
- *Guaranteed covering of young mares that often fend off the stallion despite being in season*
- *Mare and stallion can be used for other purposes during the breeding season*

Disadvantages
- *Massive interference with natural sexual behaviour*
- *Sometimes the mare is as good as raped*
- *Lower fertility rate unless covering takes place at the optimum time*
- *Long journeys may be necessary*

Artificial insemination

Nowadays, artificial insemination is carried out all over the world, but it is not permitted for Thoroughbreds. The ejaculation is separated into its mucous and non-mucous component. The non-mucous part contains the sperm. This is either used straight away to inseminate a mare or it is diluted in a transport medium and carried to the mare. Usually, the ejaculation is split into several portions and used as fresh sperm or frozen down in liquid nitrogen. Frozen, it can be kept for several years. Sperm of many deceased stallions is therefore still available.

Artificial insemination enables far more mares to be fertilised by one stallion than would be possible with natural mating. This can have disadvantages however.

If certain bloodlines and stallions are very popular and others are neglected, the genetic variation of a specific breed becomes gradually narrower and narrower. This increases the risk of hereditary diseases. It also has very little to do with natural breeding. Apart from the frustration mares and stallions must experience, more and more experts are concerned that in using such methods to breed from animals that may be naturally reluctant to mate we may be supporting a negative selection regarding sexual behaviour. The result may be that soon horses will no longer be able to mate naturally.

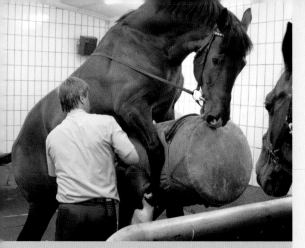

For artificial insemination, the stallion ejaculates into an artificial vagina. Often, a mare in season needs to be present to stimulate him. He then jumps onto a phantom horse. Photo: Maierhofer

Only for professionals – embryo transfer

Embryo transfer is nowadays carried out in horses too. Embryo transfer involves implanting an embryo of another (more valuable) mother into a surrogate mare. This procedure is very complicated and expensive. It should only be considered in cases when it is necessary for performance horses to continue to compete, or for mares of special value to enable them to produce more offspring than biologically possible, or for a valuable mare that cannot give birth herself tdue to health problems.

The vet or technician inserts the sperm via a long pipette into the uterus of the mare. Photo: Maierhofer

Two portions of fresh sperm are prepared for transport. Photo: Maierhofer

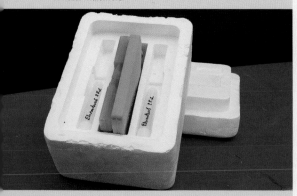

Artificial insemination

Advantages
- *Very small risk of infection*
- *No risk of mating injuries*
- *More offspring from a good stallion*
- *Availability of semen from foreign stallions*
- *No transport of horses (semen is sent by courier)*
- *Frozen semen from dead stallions can still be used*
- *Horses can be used for other purposes (e. g. competition)*

Disadvantages
- *Unnatural genetic similarity*
- *No natural sexual behaviour possible*
- *Low fertility rates*
- *Some mares do not conceive at all*

What costs are involved?

The covering fee for a stallion will vary depending upon his replacement values, his own performance and popularity. Prices between £ 200 and £ 600 are common but for competition stallions it can be as much as £ 2000 in some cases. In general, pony stallions cost rather less (£ 400 is considered expensive) whilst Thoroughbred stallions with classic winning form can cost as much as £ 100,000 – but these are unlikely to be available to the amateur owner of a single mare if you could afford it anyway!

Payment methods for covering fees also vary. Most studs require a 10 per cent non-returnable deposit (booking fee) but some also require full up-front payment with a free covering the following year if the mare does not conceive (no foal no fee or (NFFR). Others only require the outstanding 90 per cent if the mare conceives and remains in foal (NFNF) until 1 October (Oct 1 terms). This NFNF option is now far less popular with stallion owners than it was in the past because of the financial risk involved if too many infertile mares or difficult breeders are covered in one stud season. Live foal terms (one that lives at least 24 hours) is the other alternative method of identifying if the payment is due and again studs vary as to which they use. The third system of payment is the 'straight fee' which is the usual method of payment for transported semen of any kind. It is also sometimes offered as a cut rate alternative to a higher NFFR option for a live covering.

Many studs also now include a vet package in their costs, and this can be tailored to cover foaling and any necessary scans or treatment related to the covering. Expect to pay in the region of £ 300 for this.

Finally, you have to pay to have mare and foal registered with the breeding society and some also require you to be a member before you can register any animal with them. The prices for registration vary between societies but are unlikely to be less than £ 50 in total for which you will receive an equine passport including a verified pedigree and a UELN for your foal.

Dealing with mating injuries

Mating injuries can be internal or external. Tears on the outer genital area are usually detected on a visual check up. They can compromise fertility because misalignment of the vulva can increase the risk of contamination with bacteria and infections. Tears in the vaginal wall, which will allow bacteria to reach the underlying tissue in the pelvic cavity, are very serious. These can lead to a severe and often fatal peritonitis. It is therefore important to have any mating injury checked by a vet!

This is also the case if the mare appears off colour without any visible signs of injury, especially when running a temperature or showing colic symptoms immediately or up to 48 hours after covering.

Photo: Chr. Slawik

A NEW LIFE
DEVELOPS

Fertilisation

Fertilisation takes place in the mare's oviduct. The sperm has to move there actively from the uterus, which is a kind of natural competition that ensures that the strongest one gets there first and fertilises the egg.

The sperm seeks the egg cell, penetrates into its nucleus and distributes its own genetic material. This is the actual fertilisation. An egg

cell is the size of a grain of sand; a sperm cell is 100 times smaller.

The sperm consists of a head, a middle and a tail. The head contains the nucleus with the chromosomes, which is the genetic material. Horses have 64 chromosomes that are formed by 32chromosomal pairs.

Each pair contains a male and female component. The egg cell and sperm have only half of the chromosomes, i. e. 32, of all normally found in every body cell. The only exceptions are red blood cells, which have no nucleus at all.

After fertilisation, the 32 chromosomes of the egg form pairs with the 32 chromosomes of the sperm and they complete the full set of 64 chromosomes.

Has the mating been successful?

Make a note in your calendar of the mating date. Fourteen to eighteen days after the last mating, the vet can diagnose with ultrasound whether your mare has conceived. If not, the next oestrus should be imminent and can be used for another attempt. About 40 days after the first covering (plus/minus one or two days) a second ultrasonic examination should be carried out to determine whether the pregnancy is normal or not.

Development of the foal

When the embryo arrives in the uterus on day 6 after fertilisation, it measures about one mm. Two weeks later, its size is 16 mm, including the yolk that is used for nutrition. The egg membranes and first blood vessels start to develop. After day 19, the circulatory system and premature heart will have formed.

On day 50 there are first signs of head and limbs. Thirty days later, head and neck have their normal position. On day 160, the embryo has well- developed ears. As of day 220, the mane and tail will begin to grow. At this time, a warmblood foal weighs around 10 kg; at birth it weighs around 50 kg. Thoroughbred foals tend to weigh slightly less but of course most pony foals are considerably smaller, although they tend to grow at a faster rate and mature rather earlier once they are born.

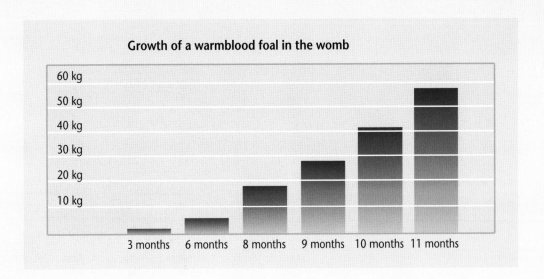

Growth of a warmblood foal in the womb

	3 months	6 months	8 months	9 months	10 months	11 months

Providing for the foetus

Like all mammals, when she is pregnant the mare provides all nutrients for the growing life and absorbs all waste products that are toxic for the foetus. This exchange takes place through the placenta, which is attached to the uterus and to which the foetus is connected via the umbilical cord. The umbilical cord contains blood vessels. Although the maternal and foetal blood systems are very close in the placenta, they do not mix.

Pregnancy testing

In horses, the fertilised egg is not firmly implanted into the uterus before the third month of pregnancy. Up to then, it floats freely inside the womb. During this time, the mare can re-absorb the embryo without showing any visible symptoms. You can therefore only be sure that the mare will stay pregnant after the first three months. An experienced vet can recognise an imminent absorption earlier, at about day 40, because the embryo will be deformed. That is the reason why a second ultrasonic examination at this time is important.

As of day 45 to 50, a pregnancy can be confirmed with a blood sample. The samples are tested for hormones that are only in the blood stream during pregnancy. After day 120, the urine will show these hormones as well, but when doing a urine test during pregnancy, it is best to use early morning urine.

Fertility problems in the mare

If the mare fails to conceive it can be for one or more of the following reasons:

The mare is too fat!
If the mare is too fat her metabolism and hormone production does not function properly.

Misalignment of the vulva
Air entering the vagina can cause infections and infertility (e. g. after examinations, mating, birth when vulva and vagina are still enlarged, or in old and badly shaped mares).

Abnormal cycle
Some mares do not come into season as long as they are suckling a foal. The hormone prolactin, responsible for the milk production, is likely to suppress other hormones regulating the cycle (e. g. follicle stimulating hormone FSH and lutein hormone LH). If you require the mare to become pregnant at all costs you may have to wean the foal. This is not a guarantee for success and on top of that, you have the further problem of a foal that is too young for weaning. It is better to be patient and wait until the following year.

Oestrus without ovulation
If the mare has an oestrus without ovulation, either the ovaries remain inactive or the follicles do not mature enough. Only a blood sample (measuring progesterone levels) or a rectal examination by a vet (manual examination of the ovaries) will reveal that an oestrus has taken place without ovulation.

Late ovulation

If the mare ovulates after the oestrus the sperm will have died so the egg cannot be fertilised.

Ovulation in the middle of the cycle

Horses quite often have an ovulation between two seasons. This can lead to a twin pregnancy, particularly when a second ovulation occurs shortly after the first one or there is a prolonged dioestrus that allows a second ovulation to occur very late in the cycle.

Prolonged intervals between cycles

Sometimes, the corpus luteum does not regress after the usual 15 days. The reasons for this are not yet fully understood. Often, an egg cell that has died can induce this problem. The mare does not come into season again and might appear to be pregnant. This is why scans, blood tests and manual examinations are so important in assessing the progress of the pregnancy.

Silent seasons

In this situation, the mare in season shows all the usual changes of her genital tract and ovaries but without any typical behavioural signs. This sometimes happens to mares that have been brought into season by artificial hormone stimulation. They can conceive as long as the season can be confirmed through veterinary examination and the mare is then covered at the right time.

Sometimes the changes in the genital tract and behaviour can occur at different times. The mare will then not accept the stallion at the critical time (i.e. 24 hours before ovulation).

Aggressive behaviour during season

This unnatural behaviour is probably more likely during a supervised mating and occurs most frequently with young mares or mares that are still feeding their first foal.

Advice

Mares are usually most fertile during moulting. By the way, clipped mares do not conceive as well! About 90 per cent of clipped mares do not become pregnant for reasons not yet known. They should only be presented to the stallion once the coat has fully re-grown.

POSSIBLE COMPLICATIONS DURING PREGNANCY

Re-absorption of the embryo during the first 12 weeks of pregnancy has already been mentioned. It is a natural stress-free way of terminating a pregnancy in order to guarantee the survival of the mare in difficult times (e. g. droughts, famine or illness).

Even towards the end of term, the growing foal can die. We need to distinguish between non-contagious and viral abortions, so any aborted foal should be examined to establish if an infection was the cause. Usually your vet will arrange for the post mortem examination to take place at an approved centre and until you have the results, you should treat the case as a viral abortion and take all necessary precautions to prevent the spread of any infections.

Causes of non-contagious abortion

Bacterial infection of the uterus

Bacteria from faeces or other sources can enter the vagina through a mis-shaped vulva at any time. They can even reach the uterus during mating or if contaminated instruments are used.

Fever

Any type of illness with fever carries the risk of inducing an abortion. Be careful when administering any kind of medication during pregnancy! Many drugs, even wormers or sedatives, can cause abortion or deformation of the foal.

Malnutrition

A rapid change in the feeding regime, sudden turn out of a previously stabled mare, feeding mouldy, rotten or contaminated food or poisonous plants, insufficient mineral and vitamin supply or lack of protein can all cause abortion.

Accidents or exhaustion

Falls, sudden exhaustion, jumping high fences or transport stress are further risks of abortion.

How to deal with viral abortion

Usually, the mare contracts this viral infection via her airways. Only a vaccination (during the third and sixth or seventh month of pregnancy) will offer protection.

Adult horses usually only show a transient fever and a clear watery nasal discharge, which often leads to the severity of the disease being under-estimated or even overlooked completely. Foals, however, can become seriously ill with a high fever, severe cough, and possible pneumonia.

In rare cases, even a vaccinated mare can abort her foal if the virus enters the uterus directly. A possible source of infection can be the semen during natural mating.

Viral abortion occurs at the end of pregnancy, and is usually sudden without any previous symptoms unlike a normal birth. In rare cases, these early foals survive for a few hours or days.

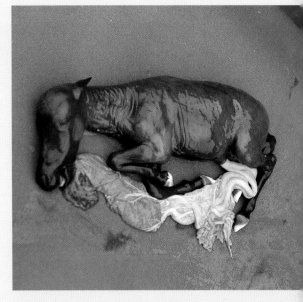

Any stillborn foal should be professionally examined to establish the reason for the abortion. Photo: Dr. Ende

Advice
If you detect milk on the mare's teats quite some time before term it can be a sign of impending abortion or birth of a premature foal. In any case, inform your vet!

In exceptional cases, both twins are born alive. They are usually smaller and weaker than other foals. Photo: Chr. Slawik

Arrange to have the dead foal and the placenta examined in order to protect other pregnant mares from an infection. The fluids are particularly infectious.

As soon as you notice that your mare might abort, isolate her from any other horses. If at all possible, move horses out of adjacent boxes. Box and stable have to be disinfected using 2 per cent alkaline solutions. Avoid any contact between your mare and other horses. Also, remember that clothes, boots and hands of people can all transmit a viral infection. If the mare aborts in the field, then the field should not be used for at least 14 days afterwards. Your vet will advise you of any other actions you need to take.

Twins

The predisposition for twin pregnancies is usually inherited. Usually, a twin pregnancy either leads to abortion between the seventh and ninth month, or one foetus dies in the womb and shrinks. If this happens then, at birth, there is often one live foal (usually a bit smaller and thinner than a normal one), and one mummified foal. There have also been rare cases when the mummified foal had grown into the body of the live one.

Young mares in particular normally feel happier and more secure in a herd. Sometimes, they are confused by the effect hormonal changes have on them and by the movements of the foal in the womb. Contact with older, experienced mares can help. Photo: Chr. Slawik

CARING FOR THE HIGHLY PREGNANT MARE

Exercise in every weather

You do not really have to change your stabling regime during the last few weeks of pregnancy. An open stable and good turn out are ideal. Fresh air, light, companions, exercise and balanced nutrition assure physical and mental well being. Stabled mares must also be turned out to exercise in fresh air every day, no matter what the weather is like. However, be careful if a mare used to being kept in a stable, just stands around in bad weather outside, as she may well become chilled which could have unfortunate results.

45

Keeping the mare fit

Although it rarely happens in the UK, it is important to remember that a light rider can ride the mare until almost the end of pregnancy. However, demanding exercise such as long gallops, hunting or jumping should not be undertaken when the mare is in foal. On the other hand light schooling can be a good idea because just standing around is very detrimental. These unfit mares often struggle when giving birth. If your mare does not exercise when turned out in a paddock or field then you might have no choice but to take her for walks.

During the last few weeks of pregnancy, the abdomen can become tremendously large. Watch out when turning your mare or walking her through doors. Also, avoid slippery, wet or frozen ground. Foto: Chr. Slawik

Content mares that feel comfortable in every way will be better prepared for their future role as mother. If a mare is not able to satisfy her natural requirements for social contact and exercise, she will often have problems during birth or with accepting and raising the foal. Photo: S. Schomburg

This is because getting cold will cost energy and this energy loss has to be compensated by food. It is better to turn out your mare frequently for shorter periods when the weather is very bad or to use a protective rug.

You also have to be careful on icy days. Uneven paddocks carry a significant accident risk. A large belly makes the mare clumsy. She can loose her balance easily resulting in possible muscle or tendon injuries or falls. Narrow doorways, sharp turns and direct contact with aggressive companions should for safety reasons be avoided, particularly towards the end of pregnancy.

FOALING

The average length of a mare's pregnancy is 11 months (340 days). Variations between 320 and 360 days are possible. Colts are usually born a few days later than fillies.

Tell the vet when your mare is due to foal and make sure that in an emergency, you can get hold of him or her at any time of the day or night.

Final preparations

If the mare has shoes on, these should be removed in time for the birth as they are a risk to the foal as well as to the helpers. The feet should be trimmed at least 4 weeks before time; otherwise it can become too difficult for the mare to balance herself whilst standing on three legs. Mare and foal should also not be disturbed by procedures like trimming during their first few days together.

Worming

The mare should be wormed 6-8 weeks before foaling and then immediately before birth. This regime prevents the foal from becoming infected during the first few days and through its dam's milk. Be careful though: the common wormers effective against bots should not be given to pregnant mares. Ask your vet for advice!

You should have these items handy for the birth:

- *Gloves*
- *Clean towels*
- *Warm water*
- *Soap*
- *Gel*
- *Iodine solution, diluted with surgical spirit*
- *Mild disinfectant*
- *Two clean and sterilized birth ropes*
- *Wound powder*
- *Pair of sharp scissors*
- *Bale twine or similar to tie up the afterbirth*
- *Baby bottle for emergencies*
- *Enema*
- *Wormer for the mare*
- *Mobile telephone (fully charged!)*
- *Telephone numbers of your vet and the National Foaling Bank*
- *Trailer or horse box for emergencies*

Watch your mare particularly carefully during the last few days of pregnancy. Clean her coat and genital area regularly and remove all sticky material that builds up between the teats because it can be a source of bacterial infection for the foal. Do not manipulate the udder as this can cause premature milk flow. Valuable colostrum will then drip into the straw and be lost to the foal.

The importance of peace and quiet

A mare giving birth needs to feel absolutely secure. Many mares prepare to foal when people are absent. That is especially true for native breeds, which usually give birth outside on their own. Mares can speed up the birth or postpone it for a few days to ensure optimum conditions of safety. Too many checks and general noise can therefore lead to a delay in the birth process. This effect is called 'psychogenic influence on the uterus activity'. It describes either the increase or a complete standstill in uterus contractions. As the wild horse is hunted by predators, this ability can guarantee its survival. Under the care of humans, the control over labour, although no longer necessary, is still present and can even harm the foal if the mare has only a short quiet moment and starts to push hastily. You must therefore avoid frequent interruptions at the time of birth. To help you keep visits to her to a minimum use a foaling alarm that will react to an increase in the moisture of the skin or to the mare lying down, or if possible a video camera so that you can observe developments from a distance.

Signs of impending birth

First signs of an impending birth are an increase of udder size and drops of milk on the teats, which is known as 'waxing up'. In some mares, these can appear up to 7 days before the actual birth, in others only shortly beforehand. A few hours before birth, the vulva will swell and become moist and the pelvic ligaments soften. The mare's rump will not look round any more but more like that of a cow. The closer the birth, the more restless the mare will become. She will begin to pace, chew her hay nervously or start to sweat or shiver. There are, however, always some mares that start to foal without any warning signs. Others show these symptoms although the foal has only changed its position in the womb.

The normal birth

There are three stages to a normal birth;

1. **First stage – dilation of cervix**
2. **Second stage – pushing and birth**
3. **Third stage – delivery of the placenta**

The first stage is not visible from the outside. About 4 hours before birth, the activity inside the womb increases. The resulting labour might appear similar to a mild colic. The mare is restless, paws the ground, sweats, lies down and gets up again, relieves herself frequently. During this stage, the foal turns round and the amniotic sack is pushed towards the cervix. The pelvis widens and the waters usually break when the amniotic sack leaves the vagina. Most

Drops on the teats (wax) are a sign of imminent birth. Photo: Dr. Ende

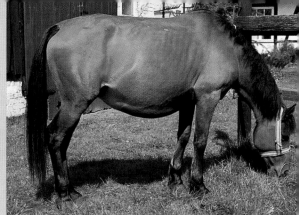

The pelvic ligaments soften. Photo: Dr. Ende

At the beginning of the second stage, most mares lie down. Photo: Dr. Ende

The head and front legs of the foal are still covered by the membranes. Photo: Dr. Ende

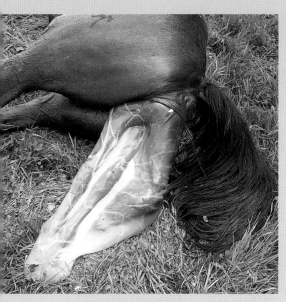

Strong contractions push the foal out. Photo: Dr. Ende

As soon as the shoulders are out, the rest will usually follow with the next contraction. Photo: Dr. Ende

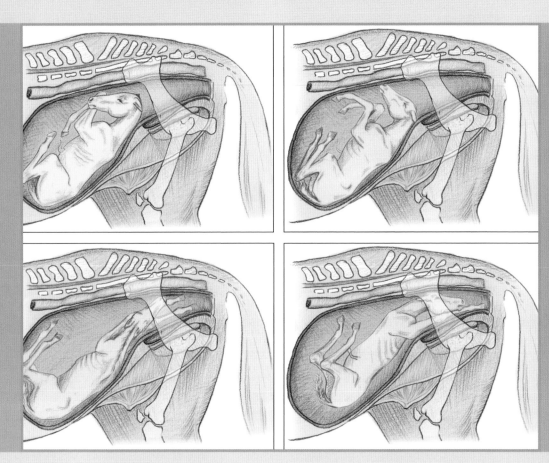

Change in position of the foal during a normal birth process.

mares foal while lying down. If your mare foals in a stable you should have sufficient bedding along the walls to offer the mare maximum space to stretch out.

A normal birth process does not take longer than 10 to 30 minutes from when the time the waters break. Do not interfere! As long as there are no complications, the mare will manage by herself.

Once the waters break, the mare will start to push. The mare will lie on her side and have strong contractions (two or three contractions every 2–3 minutes). She might get up in between and change her position. Labour can be very hard work. The mare might even throw herself on the floor and groan and sweat.

The amniotic sack will now appear and the foal's head and extended front legs will become visible. Pushing the head through the pelvis is the most difficult part for the mare. After that, it usually takes only seconds until the foal comes out. The membranes tear during this stage and thus allow the foal to breathe. If this does not happen as soon as the foal is born it will move and shake its head in order to free itself from any tissue. When the mare gets up the umbilical cord will tear at its predetermined point.

The afterbirth then loosens its attachment from the uterus and is usually pushed out within 15 to 120 minutes after birth. This process can also induce some mild colic signs. In order to avoid the mare stepping on the protruding afterbirth and tearing it off, you should tie it up using bale twine.

Once the placenta has come out you should check it thoroughly to make sure that it is complete. If you are unsure if everything has come out fill it up with water. You will then be able to detect any holes easily. Bits of retained afterbirth can lead to infections. If you suspect that the placenta is not complete you should inform your vet immediately.

Inducing birth

This is not often necessary in equine births, but occasionally the vet has to do this if the mare had problems at previous births, is ill, or the birth process stops or similar. You should never consider asking the vet to do this for your own convenience (e. g. to avoid too many night watches). Despite all medical advances, there is always a risk to the foal with this procedure.

The natural birth process starts when the unborn foal indicates to the mother that it is now mature enough to fend for itself outside the protective womb. It is impossible to test the degree of maturity of the foal before birth at the moment and foals born (or induced) too early can be premature and therefore weak. The lungs, for example, only mature during the last two weeks before birth.

Still wet from the birth, this Arab foal curiously checks out its surroundings. Photo: N. Sachs

THE NEW BORN FOAL

Caring for the very young foal

Even before the umbilical cord ruptures, a healthy foal begins to breathe. Leave the mare and foal in peace and if possible, do not interfere with the cord, even if it does not tear straight away. The foal needs every drop of maternal blood after the stress of birth. Wash and disinfect your hands thoroughly. Grab the umbilical cord close to the visible site where it is meant to rupture and twist it with your hands until it tears off. Dip the cord into iodine solution (that is best done using a small glass).

As soon as the foal has arrived, the mare will start to lick it dry. This not only helps to remove the membrane but also increases the cir-

culation of the skin. She will also take in the
foal's smell at this time, which helps to build
up an intense bond between the mare and her
foal.

Imprinting by the mare

Every foal needs to learn who its mother is.
This process is called imprinting. It only takes
place during an early sensitive phase, which,
in horses, is very short. As soon as it is established it cannot be reversed. Disturbances can
compromise this process and the foal can imprint on other beings or even objects. This is
why, in the wild, the mare isolates her baby
foal from the rest of the herd as best she can.
While the mare is able to identify her foal clear-
ly after half an hour, imprinting in the foal can
take up to two days. Only when it is completed will the foal actively follow its mother.

The imprinting process is very important for
the development of the foal. Disturbances by
other horses as well as people should be avoided at all costs. You should restrain yourself to
observing the mare and foal from a distance

1 kg bran
1 kg crushed oats
300 g boiled linseed
300 g maze flakes

Mix the ingredients with 50 g of salt and a
litre of water (or fruit tea) and bring it to the
boil briefly. Leave it to cool and swell (stirring
occasionally) and then add 500 g of mineral
supplement. Feed it luke warm. Do not keep
it for longer than one day and remove all left-
overs thoroughly from the trough.

instead of falling for the temptation to stroke
the foal constantly. Foals that are handled too
much early on can develop into thugs, as they
never learned to respect people.

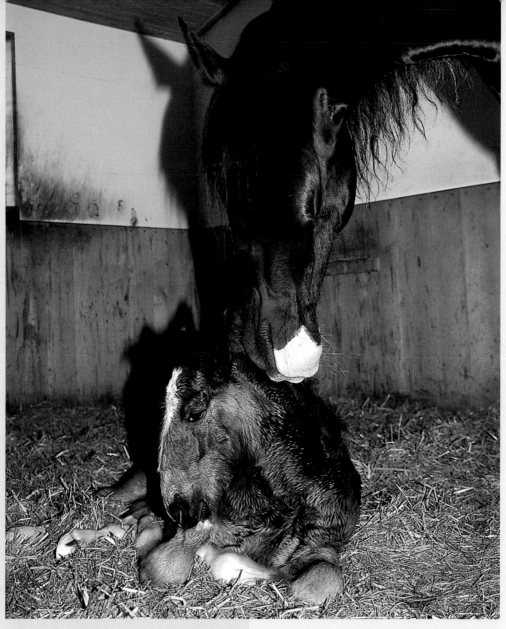

Happy moments: Mother and foal get to know each other.
Photo: Chr. Slawik

Human imprinting

A few years ago, a new method of imprinting was developed in the USA. Its aim was to use the sensitive phase of the foal and imprint it on to people as well as on to its mother. Thus, the foal would recognise humans as members of its own species and tolerate being handled, which practitioners believe made future handling and training easier. In this procedure, the foal is held to the ground and touched everywhere until it accepts this without resistance.

The relationship between mare and foal can be disturbed if the foal imprints on to someone else. Photo: Chr. Slawik

It is important, however, that it does not feel fear.

This is where the major problem lies with this controversial method. Critics believe that these foals turn into lifelong 'losers' and 'weaklings' without character. Other behavioural problems can also develop later in life.

Changing behaviour in the mare

It is normal for a mare to react aggressively towards people or other animals during the im-printing phase. Just keep your distance and leave mother and foal alone. After about 10 days, the mare should be back to her normal behaviour. If this does not happen, you should establish your higher rank once again through a dominant attitude. Hold the mare by a rope and make her go sideways or backwards repeatedly. But please be cautious! Some mares change significantly after the birth and they no longer show any respect, even to people with whom they are familiar.

55

WHEN SOMETHING GOES WRONG

Do not worry too much! Assistance is necessary in only about 5 per cent of births in horses. However, in order for you to be prepared in the rare circumstance when something does go wrong the following guidelines should be of help to you.

Advice

If you have to assist the mare during foaling always remember to wash and disinfect your hands thoroughly before and after! Even better, wear sterile gloves.

The amniotic sack doesn't break

In this case, you have to open the sack as if you don't there will be a risk of the foal suffocating. Carefully free the head and nostrils of mucus by wiping it from the outside of the nostrils.

Avoid sticking your fingers into the foal's mouth as you could introduce an infection. If the foal has a problem breathing because it has aspirated fluid it needs to be held up quickly by its hind legs so that the fluid can drain through the mouth and nostrils. If it does not breathe by itself you can lift a front leg and thus expand the lungs, which often encourage spontaneous breathing. Only in an emergency should you consider pouring cold water on the back of the head, and if you have to do this don't forget to dry the foal afterwards with clean straw.

The birth process ceases

If head and front legs are visible but the birth process has stopped you can gently pull the legs to help.

It is important to pull backwards and downwards and only during a contraction. As the

56

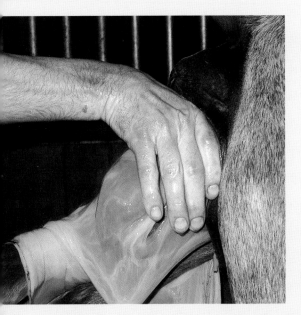

Photo: Dr. Ende

must use gel or soap as a lubricant when doing this and once you make contact with the bent or trapped leg it is often possible to extend it. If you cannot do this you must contact your vet straight away and try to make the mare get up so that she stops pushing for the time being (i. e. until the vet arrives to help).

Alternatively, if the front legs do not protrude equally you can pull them until they are both showing the same length. If that is not possible you must make the mare get up as this often causes the foal to slide back into the uterus. Get help and while waiting, make the mare stand with her back end raised (e. g. by piling up straw on the ground). However, you have to be careful if the foal's chest is already in the vagina, because in this situation, you must not interrupt the birth but actually speed it up by pulling the foal carefully (as described above), as otherwise the foal can easily choke.

vulva can easily tear (especially in young mares), push the tight skin carefully over the foal with your hand.

Breach presentation

In this case, the foal lies back to front. Inform your vet immediately as breached births are rarely without complications.

One leg is trapped

If you can see only one leg next to the head and the birth has stopped push your clean and disinfected hand past the other side of the head until you reach the second front leg. You

The foal is too big for the mare

If the foal is too big in relation to the mare's pelvis it can lead to a difficult birth, and this sometimes happens when the foal is overdue. It can get stuck in the pelvis and might choke or the umbilical chord could rupture too soon.

The mare needs assistance if

- *Red tissue appears instead of the blue-white amnion. This is the placenta and it needs to be opened immediately.*
- *The inner layer of the amnion does not appear.*
- *Head and legs do not appear.*
- *There are no contractions or the foal does not come out despite contractions.*
- *The mare gets up and down frequently while pushing.*
- *The foal is in the wrong position, which is always the case when both front legs and the head do not appear first.*

Torn uterus

In rare cases, the foal moves its legs violently while being pushed through the pelvis. This can give the mare severe internal injuries. If the mare shows colic symptoms after birth, her mucus membranes are pale and she sweats up, an internal injury could have occurred. Call your vet immediately and try to milk as much colostrum as possible (see also the section entitled 'Colostrum: the natural vaccine') because you might lose your mare due to internal bleeding. Also, prepare transport in case you need to travel the mare and foal or collect a foster mare.

Retention of the afterbirth

About 2–3 hours after birth, the cervix begins to close. If the placenta has not been expelled by then you need to inform your vet. This is because there is a high risk of toxaemia leading to severe illness (uterus infection or laminitis) in this situation.

Damaged vertebrae or pelvis in the mare

If the mare shows an abnormal gait after birth (e. g. shortened strides in one hind leg, altered rhythm or lameness), have her examined to establish whether the birth has caused a luxation or dislocation of some vertebrae or the sacro-ileac joint.

Aggressive behaviour of the mare

If the mare shows aggression against other horses, it is best to move them somewhere else. Some young mares or mares that are normally kept in public livery or on a training yard can show aggression towards the foal because they do not recognise the foal for what it is. In this case, some try to kick the newborn, others will not let it suckle and bite it when it approaches.

Usually it is just inexperience, fear and pain from the birth that causes this behaviour. Under no circumstances should the mare be punished. Try to calm her down, hold her gently

and reward her for letting the foal get close and suckle. She will then learn to associate the newborn with something positive. The first suckling alone is usually very pleasant as the pressure in the udder will decrease. It also leads to a release of endorphins ('happiness' hormones).

Disturbances immediately after the birth can also upset the mother/foal relationship. Sometimes the mare will aim her aggression against her foal instead of the real cause.

Aggression without detectable reason is quite rare, but mares that show this behaviour must never be used for breeding again.

If a mare does not accept her foal, Bach remedies may help. Various experts know the correct mixture. Apply 10 to 15 drops several times a day to the forehead of the mare.

If you do not know anyone who can prescribe the correct mixture for your horse you can try the following Bach flowers (diluted in 3 parts of water and 1 part of alcohol)

Star of Bethlehem – against trauma
Crab apple – when rejecting the foal
Holly – against aggression
Mimulus – against fear
Rock Rose – against panic reactions
Olive – against exhaustion

The newborn foal instinctively recognises the angle of the abdomen and hind legs in order to find the udder quickly.
Photo: Maierhofer

WHEN THE FIRST EXCITEMENT IS OVER

Checking that the foal is healthy

If the birth has gone well you should leave mare and foal alone for a while. Be patient and do not try to lift the foal and guide it to the udder. The foal should get there by itself within the first hour. Under no circumstances should you milk the mare and offer it to the foal in a bottle. In a healthy foal, this will only make it harder for the foal to accept the udder. If you have a weak foal, bottle feeding alone will not help anyway.

After 2 hours at the most, a healthy foal will be up and will have found the udder. The suckling reflex is present from about 20 minutes after the birth. You can see how the foal forms a groove with its tongue and you will hear it suckle. When the milk flows, foals swish their tails vividly. With each drink, the foal will find the udder more easily.

Suckling provides nutrition but also has a soothing effect on the foal. If a foal is frightened or separated from its mother, it will immediately start to drink as soon as it is with its mother again.

Advice
Newborn foals drink four to seven times per hour. Observe this closely during the first few hours. If the foal tries to drink more often, it might point towards a problem with the mare (e. g. she is not producing enough milk), or in rare cases it might signify a health problem with the foal.
No milk should flow out of a healthy foal's nostrils.

Colostrum: the natural vaccine

Contrary to what happens in humans, a foal does not receive antibodies from its mother. The so-called placenta barrier prevents antibodies from the maternal blood reaching the foetal circulation, so the foal is born without any protection against disease. Furthermore, the foal's ability to produce its own antibodies does not develop until it is 3 months of age. During the first three days of lactation the mare therefore produces colostrums containing particularly high amounts of antibodies (immunoglobulin). Also, the intestines of the newborn foal allow penetration of large protein molecules, but this permeability decreases gradually after the first 36 hours. After that, immunoglobulin is digested, like any other proteins, so time is therefore crucial. If the foal does not receive sufficient colostrum during this period it will be prone to infection. Experienced breeders always freeze a small amount of colostrum for use in emergencies. They are then well-prepared if a mare does not have enough milk or dies at birth. Colostrum should be defrosted slowly in warm water; not put it in a microwave to thaw out.

As colostrum contains antibodies against the most important diseases in the mare's environment, do not move the mare to a new yard during the last month of pregnancy. She should also be moved to the foaling box early.

Pure power

Colostrum is particularly rich in proteins and energy. Colostrum has 37.6 Mega joules (MJ) per kg which is about three times more than oats (ca. 13.1 MJ per kg). The energy content decreases gradually when the milk production goes up.

The suckling reflex is inherited. Photo: Maierhofer

During the first few days, foals need a considerable amount of sleep. Plenty of clean bedding in the stable is therefore important. Photo: Maierhofer

The importance of hygiene

Stable hygiene is of utmost importance, especially during the first few days after birth. Under no circumstances should the foal lick dirty objects (that includes dirty hands). Infectious foal diseases are much rarer when foals are kept on pasture for that very reason. Daily mucking out of stabled mares and foals is therefore absolutely essential.

Eating droppings in the first few days

It is normal for a new-born foal to eat fresh droppings from its mother. This helps the foal to develop a healthy gut flora. Old faeces, however, especially if they are contaminated with worms, are unhealthy and can induce severe diarrhoea.

Worm your mare a day after the birth with a wormer containing ivermectine. This helps eliminate small strongyles that can also live in the udder. If they are left untreated, the foal can become infected through suckling and develop severe diarrhoea after a few days.

The mare and foal should be treated against roundworm infections when the foal is 3–8 weeks old and this needs to be repeated every 8 weeks until the foal is weaned.

When to feed extra milk

If the mare does not have enough milk or does not accept the foal, you have no choice but to bottle feed the foal. There are various commercial milk powders made especially for foals. Your vet can advise you which one is best in your case or you can consult the Internet.

Cow's milk is not really acceptable because of its contents. You should only use it in an extreme emergency, and then it should be prepared as follows: 2 parts of milk diluted with 1 part of sterilised water. Add one tablespoon of lactose or glucose per litre. Feed the mixture luke warm. Be careful not to bend the foal's head backwards as fluid can get into its lungs.

Important advice when feeding milk powder: the minerals in the powder of the mixture are heavier than the rest so they sink to the bottom of the bag or bucket. Therefore, you must turn the bag every few days! If you don't, your foal will not get enough minerals during the first few days and an overdose towards the end.

Your mare does not have enough milk

Insufficient milk production can have the following causes:
- *The mare is overweight.*
- *The mare is ill.*
- *The mare does not drink enough.*
- *The mare is malnourished, especially lacking proteins.*
- *The foal is too weak or ill and does not suckle often enough.*

The size of the udder does not necessarily give an indication about how much milk a mare produces. A relatively small udder should therefore not worry you as long as the foal develops well. Pay attention to whether the foal drinks from both sides of the udder. If it does not touch one side it can be an indication of a problem in this half, or the untouched side can develop mastitis caused by the retained milk.

Allergic reaction to colostrum

In rare cases, a foal can have an allergic reaction to the colostrum. This happens when the mare builds up antibodies against the foal during pregnancy that are then transmitted via the milk. They penetrate the intestines of the foal, reach the blood stream and cause severe reactions: the foal shivers, becomes weaker and weaker and develops icterus. If this happens you will have to feed the foal with substitute milk (the substitute must contain antibodies) for about 5 days. The mare should be hand milked during this time to assure continuous milk production. Destroy the milk or freeze it in case of an emergency with another foal. After a few days, the foal can return to its mother without any risk, as now the antibodies can no longer penetrate the intestinal wall.

Mastitis

If a mare suddenly stops allowing her foal to drink, she could be suffering from mastitis. Mastitis can also develop during pregnancy. The udder becomes sore, hot, hard and starts to swell. As horses have two openings in each teat the udder cannot be flushed like in cows. Treatment has to be systemic (i.e. by injections or in the feed). Call your vet in any case. Untreated mastitis can lead to irreversible damage of the udder. Also, the milk is contaminated with bacteria and the milk production goes down, which is harmful to the foal as well.

Death of the mare

If the mare dies during or shortly after the birth, raising the foal using a foster mare is certainly the ideal solution, even if you have to take the foal somewhere else. Vets or breed societies can give you contact details of breeders with a suitable foster mare as can the National Foaling Bank, who are also able to offer practical advice on coping with a rejecting or aggressive mare. At the beginning, the foal needs to be fed every 2 hours; at night, at least every 3 hours; then later every 4 hours. On day 1, the foal should drink at least 1.5 litres of milk per day. Then gradually increase this amount. After week 1, the foal should drink about 15 litres divided into six meals.

Bottle fed foals often lack vitamins A and D, which sometimes leads to rickets. Ask your vet about vitamin supplements that you can mix into the substitute milk.

Bottle feeding a foal is not easy. Specialists can offer professional help. Photo: Chr. Slawik

Specialised yards can also offer intensive care for orphaned or sick foals. Photo: Dallmer

Be aware, however, of excessive vitamin supply. A vitamin D overdose can negatively influence the bone structure. These foals are more prone to develop fractures.

Covering the mare again

If you plan to carry on breeding from your mare do not cover her on the very first oestrus after birth (about 9 days afterwards) but rather wait until the second one (three weeks later). The rumour that the first season is particularly successful for conception is still widely believed, although scientific research does not support it. In reality, only about 40 per cent of mares covered in the first season conceive and subsequently give birth to a healthy foal. Problems during pregnancy and re-absorption are far more common in a 'foal heat' pregnancy than they are in those resulting from later matings. This is because the main function of the first oestrus is to cleanse the uterus, which produces fluids that act as an anti-inflammatory at this time. Also, a foal can cope with travel better at 5–6 weeks of age than a few days after being born.

DISEASES OF THE FOAL

Diseases in all youngsters usually develop faster and are more dramatic than in adults. It is therefore important to prevent rather that treat an illness. If the foal gets ill it is crucial to recognise this soon and to provide or get the necessary support very quickly. Listlessness, fatigue and apathy are the alarm signals! Even if the foal seems only slightly off colour you should take its temperature. The normal body temperature of a newborn foal is initially as high as 39 deg C (adult horses 37.5–38.5 deg C). A 14 day old foal should not have a temperature of more than 38.5 deg C.

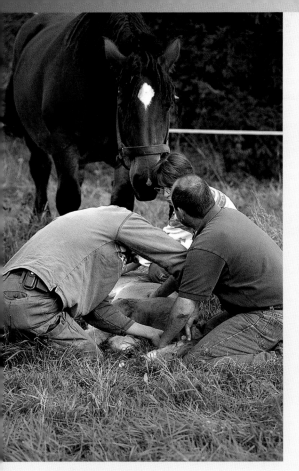

Sick foals need expert help quickly.
Photo: Slawik

Meconium retention

A foal produces 500 to 800 g of meconium within the first 12 hours. It usually passes this without any problems because of the laxative effect of colostrum. After that, the foal produces golden brown milk faeces. In some cases, however, the meconium forms a very hard lump, which cannot be passed. The meconium is stuck and dries out more and more. The foal cannot pass any new faeces either. A dangerous impaction develops. Remember, colts are more affected than fillies because they have a narrower pelvis. It is also more common in foals that were born later than expected.

The affected foal is restless and swishes its tail. It then starts to roll and turns its head towards its abdomen. The symptoms are similar to colic. In between these spells it often drinks as normal.

Advice
A sufficient sodium supply in the mare's feed before birth can reduce the risk of meconium retention in the foal. Add 40 g of salt, preferably with iodine, to the feed.

Meconium is the firm, dark brown and sticky mass that is produced by the foal during the pre-natal phase. It consists of dead intestinal cells, hairs, fat, juices and bile.
Photo: Slawik

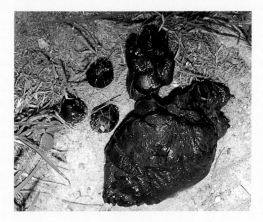

Frequent rolling in the first days can be a sign of retained meconium. Photo: Chr. Slawik

Many breeders give all foals a mixture of mare's milk and liquid paraffin via a baby bottle to prevent the retention of meconium. It is important to wash your hands beforehand. If the meconium does not pass spontaneously an enema can also help. Be very careful when administering the enema as the foal's intestinal membranes are very delicate. Never use hard objects. If you want to check with your finger whether any meconium is stuck make sure your fingernails are short and round and use lots of lubrication on your finger or glove. Do not apply too much pressure when administering the enema as the intestines can tear. If the restlessness and colic symptoms continue after the meconium has passed, or generally for more than 3 hours, call your vet.

Advice
If the vet examines your foal or takes its temperature, restrain it by having one arm around its chest and the other one around the hindquarters just below the tail.

Joint-ill

Joint-ill is still the most common cause of death in foals. The infection happens during the first few days through the navel, and sometimes already exists in the womb of the mare. The first symptoms become apparent within a few days. The foal is listless, does not drink and has swollen joints. It also often has a high temperature. If joint-ill is recognised early the vet can usually save the foal but most often there will be subsequent damage (e. g. damage to the cartilage of the joint). You can have your mare vaccinated in the eighth month of pregnancy to ensure the foal receives the antibodies it needs to fight joint-ill with the milk but that is not always successful either. For this reason, many vets inject a long-acting antibiotic during the first few hours after birth. Latest research, however, strongly discourages this as profuse fatal diarrhoea can develop after such a treatment!

It is better to use a so-called live vaccine that is produced using the blood of an older healthy stable mate, because this has been shown to have the highest amount of antibodies against all the stable-specific infectious agents. The production of such a vaccine takes about three weeks, so it needs to be started well ahead of the birth. The vaccine can be stored in a fridge or be frozen for quite some time. The foal is then vaccinated on day 1 and day 10. A blood transfusion from an older donor gelding is possible as well.

Iron injections can improve the blood production. However, although they are often recommended, they are usually unnecessary and can even be dangerous. They are only neces-sary when an actual lack of iron has been diagnosed. Talk to your vet about it.

You can ask your vet to carry out a quick test to check whether your foal has enough joint-ill antibodies in its blood. The vet will take a small blood sample and check the immunoglobulin content. It is important to carry out this test as soon as possible – ideally within the first twelve to 24 hours after birth.

Quick immunoglobulin tests should not upset the mare or foal in any way. Photo: Chr. Slawik

Diarrhoea

There are several different types of diarrhoea

Non-contagious intestinal infection in new-born foals

Non-contagious diarrhoea, which develops within the first few days, can be profuse with yellow faeces but without a strong smell. Body temperature remains normal. It is usually cured with a few days of dieting and subsequent controlled and reduced suckling. Only in very persistent cases will the vet prescribe any medication. Be careful when administering liquid drugs. The horse's larynx easily allows fluids to get into the lungs and they can cause dangerous aspiration and/or pneumonia. Do not bend the foal's head backwards!

Contagious intestinal infection

This infection is associated with greyish, smelly diarrhoea, often with blood, which weakens the foal. The affected animals run a temperature, are listless and dull. This disease is dangerous and very contagious. Call your vet immediately!

Physiological (normal) diarrhoea on day 9

This type of diarrhoea is induced by the mare's oestrus and does not normally require treatment. It is a good idea to cover the foal's anal area with Vaseline during this time to prevent hair loss.

Diarrhoea around day 9 can also be caused by an infection with strongyles through the milk.

Diarrhoea in foals can also have other causes:
- The mare has too much milk and the foal cannot empty the udder. In this case, the consistency of the remaining milk will change and bacteria will start to grow in it. In these cases, you must reduce the mare's food, especially replacing fresh grass with hay.
- Eating faeces (e. g. because of vitamin or mineral deficiency)
- Licking stable walls, objects, salt licks and dirty hands.
- Turn out on freshly fertilised pastures.
- Easy access to an automatic drinker.

- Worm infestation. Even if worms do not always cause diarrhoea, they do compromise the foal's development and can lead to a higher susceptibility to illness. A faecal sample is often inconclusive as the worms are still in their larval stage and do not produce eggs. Apart from tapeworms, only the worm eggs can be found in a sample. Special wormers for foals can be administered from the third week.

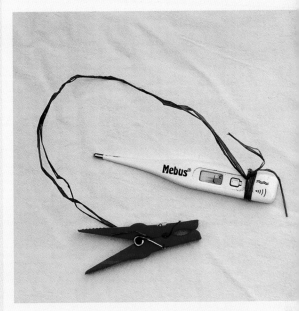

To take a foal's temperature, clip the thermometer to its tail using a bit of string and a clothes peg). Photo: N. Künzel

Advice
Foals with diarrhoea need intensive care. They dehydrate quickly and sometimes need to be put on a drip.

Infectious arthritis

Like joint-ill, infectious arthritis is often confused with lameness and you may think that the foal has been kicked or suffered some sort of similar injury. Always check the foal's joint when detecting any kind of stiffness or swelling especially on the hind legs, and take the temperature and observe its general well being. Usually, the hocks are affected first, then the knees and stifles. The joints are hot and

swollen. Sometimes, other symptoms like coughing, diarrhoea or a swelling of the navel are present. With progression of the illness, the foals will become listless and wish to lie down without moving.

Navel infection

Foals suffering from a navel infection have spells of fever and become increasingly weaker. The navel is swollen and painful. Navel infections can develop into other problems (e. g. joint-ill) or can be caused by primary diseases. In any case, the vet needs to treat the foal.

Advice
Check the navel regularly for the first few weeks after birth, but do not touch it as this can cause an infection as well.

Hernia

An umbilical hernia usually presents as a pea-sized swelling around the navel, which appears at the age of about four weeks. It sometimes induces colic-like symptoms that are an indication that a piece of intestine is trapped in the hernia. You should always have a vet examine a hernia. Local applications or a minor surgical procedure on a standing foal will often resolve the problem.

Ruptured bladder

If a foal gets crushed during birth this can cause a bladder rupture, especially in male foals. During the first two days, the foals do not show any obvious symptoms. Urine is not passed properly and flows partly into the abdomen. This leads to a slow intoxication. Always be aware of prolonged resting periods, reduced drinking, listlessness and colic symptoms after day two. The abdomen can become enlarged. If the problem is diagnosed early these foals have a fair chance as the rupture can be surgically repaired.

Upper airway infection

When suffering from an upper airway infection, initially foals do not cough but over time they become short-breathed and later develop a purulent nasal discharge. If the nostrils become blocked a loud breathing noise can be heard. The foals usually do not run a temperature nor do they have swollen lymph nodes. Their general well being is not compromised.

These symptoms frequently disappear spontaneously. However, whilst the foal is ill you must pay utmost attention to stable hygiene and make sure that there is a good air supply in the stable. Clean the nostrils regularly and disinfect all contaminated objects (and walls) that the foal touches on a daily basis.

The foal needs plenty of fresh air so it should be turned out as long as it has no fever – but only if the weather is good! In order to be sure of the diagnosis, call your vet at the first signs of a cough.

Pneumonia

Pneumonia can develop after any type of airway infection if bacteria enter the lungs or after aspiration of fluids. It is always life-threatening. Call your vet as soon as possible.

Sometimes, foals run a fever for several weeks without the medication having any effect and if this is the cause then permanent damage is a high possibility.

Strangles

Strangles is a bacterial infection, caused by streptococcus equi and it can affect horses of any age, although older horses rarely become ill because they have often already developed an immunity to it. The infected animal develops a high temperature, is listless and eats very little. The lymph nodes in the head area fill with pus, which also causes problems swallowing. Some foals can only swallow a small portion of the water or milk and the rest flows out of the nostrils. If the breathing becomes laboured as well the abscesses need to be lanced by the vet.

Strangles can develop as a complication after a harmless viral infection. The bacteria are transmitted to other animals through the air but also by people. The pus from bursting or lanced abscesses is particularly contagious.

In addition to veterinary medication, preventative vaccination is increasingly popular, especially in mixed yards. Remedies like plant packs and bay leaf oil are also beneficial.

Strangles needs to be treated aggressively in order to avoid the bacteria spreading to internal organs and causing serious complications. It can lead to:
- Poor growth
- Whistling
- Chronic lameness
- Pleurisy
- Eye infections, which can lead to blindness
- Guttural pouch infection
- Paralysis of the swallowing reflex
- Silent 'carriers' status, in which a previously infected horse can spread infection even when apparently healthy

The best way to avoid malnutrition in the foal is to supply the mare with high quality feed during pregnancy and lactation and add correctly calculated amounts of vitamins, minerals and trace elements. Photo: S. Schomburg

CORRECT FEEDING OF MARE AND FOAL

Many lengthy books have been written about equine nutrition. However, most often they deal almost exclusively with the feeding of mature riding horses and ponies, and the nutritional requirements of mares and foals differ in several important ways, which are outlined below.

Feeding during pregnancy and lactation

Pregnancy and the subsequent period of lactation are a big challenge for the body. Their effect on nutrition is totally different to that of sport or other similar activities of mature horses and ponies.

Like all horses, the food requirements of the pregnant mare have two components: maintenance and performance requirements. Maintenance means providing enough energy to sustain the body mass and all the body functions. Its value depends on type, weight, age and environmental influences (in particular climate and temperature) and it is relatively consistent in each brood mare.

Performance requirements can be split into four parts:

1. First part of pregnancy (first to seventh month)
2. End stage of pregnancy (eight to eleventh month)
3. Lactating mare (feeding a foal)
4. Empty mare (after weaning)

The quality and balance of the various feeds is more important than the amount. Overfeeding is detrimental. Overweight mares do not conceive as well as slim ones. High quality hay is an essential part of the feeding regime and it cannot be replaced by anything else.

The danger of over feeding

This risk applies to feeding in general but especially for brood mares.

Obesity reduces fertility and fat mares sometimes never conceive. Non-pregnant and non-lactating mares should be well covered but not fat when taken to the stud.

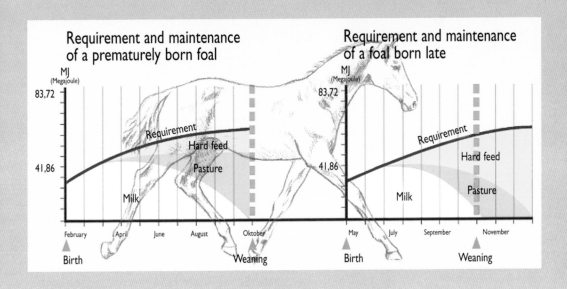

This means that you should be able to feel the ribs but not see them, although the rump should still be round. Mares that are not worked only need to maintain their body weight, but make sure that the feed has a good calcium: phosphorus ratio (Ca:P 1.5 to 1.7:1) and also contains sufficient vitamin A and E, both of which are very important for fertility. The body can produce vitamin A out of a provitamin A (beta-carotin) and all green plants as well as carrots and sugar beet contain beta-carotin.

With regard to feeding, mating later in the season is more beneficial because the pregnant and lactating mare will have plenty of good grass available. This will make feeding the mare and her foal much easier as they can be turned out to graze, which is difficult to arrange for an early-season foal.

Mares out on good grass during the early stages of pregnancy do not usually require additional feed, apart from a mineral supplement.

During the first eight weeks of pregnancy, avoid any change in feeding regime. Be careful if the grazing season starts just then! Turning out the mare onto fresh young new-season grass for the first time is definitely not recommended because the embryo is extremely sensitive to environmental change at this time but it does not yet need increased nutrition.

Increased nutritional needs in the final stage of pregnancy

Apart from plenty of exercise, the dam's nutrition is the most important factor for the development of the unborn foal. A lack of certain nutrients can affect various organs without the foal showing any obvious signs at birth. It has also been shown recently, that malnutrition of the mare can have an effect on more than one subsequent generation.

The last two or three months of pregnancy are the most important in this respect as the foal grows significantly during this time. Make sure that your feeding regime is closely matched to the mare's needs during this period and adjust it so she neither puts on nor looses weight. Feed sufficient high quality hay (i. e. 15 per cent crude protein content) up to 0.5 kg per 100 kgs of her body weight.

Sugar beet (thoroughly soaked) as well as boiled linseed stimulates gut movement. Pay even more attention to the quality of the feed during this final stage of pregnancy than at any other time.

You also have to bear in mind that as it grows, the embryo of the foal will compress the digestive organs more and more. Most mares eat much less towards the end of pregnancy and therefore you should feed more concentrate in small and frequent meals, making sure that it includes a sufficient supply of minerals, vitamins and trace elements.

If you are inexperienced with feeding regimes it is better to use a special brood mare mix. When mixing feeds yourself there is the danger of feeding too much or not enough, and both can lead to serious skeletal damage in mare and foal. Problems in later years often have their roots here.

Advice
A few days before birth, cut down on hay in order to relieve the digestive system. Make sure that the mare does not compensate this by eating more straw!

Feeding following foaling

Do not overfeed your mare during the first few days after the birth her milk production will be increasing only slowly. Gradually increase the amount of feed up to 1.5 kg of hard feed per 100 kg of body weight of the mare. Feed the concentrate in at least five portions per day. Also, feed at least 1.5 kg of hay per 100 kg of body weight. This can be reduced with increased turn out on pasture.

A mix for highly pregnant or lactating mares should contain:

Calcium	1 to 2 per cent
Phosphorus	0.4 to 0.5 per cent
Sodium	0.2 to 0.3 per cent
Vitamin A	30,000 IU
Vitamin E	300 mg
Vitamin D	3,000 IU
Iodine	< 1 mg

Advice
If the mare has little appetite or does not produce enough milk, malt or sugar beet (mixed in with the feed) has shown to be beneficial.

At no other time is the mare's requirement for protein, energy and minerals as high as when she is feeding a foal.
Photo: Chr. Slawik

As mares and grazing both vary greatly you should have your basic feeds (grass, hay, silage) analysed and have exact portions calculated based upon this. You can find out more information about this in specialised articles or by using the services of an independent nutritionist (not a feed company representative) who will often use dedicated computer programs to develop individualised feeding schedules for each horse.

The costs of having an individual feeding regime calculated are well worth it, as you want to provide optimal nutrition to your mare and foal and use the expensive feeds efficiently.

Consequences for your foal if an incorrect feeding programme is chosen

Insufficient energy content	Embryo absorption
Lack of sodium	Meconium retention
Iodine (lack/surplus)	Weak foal
Lack of selenium	Weak immune system, muscular problems
Surplus of selenium	Hoof deformation, liver damage
Lack of copper	Limb deformation, blood and nerve disorders,
Lack of vitamin A	Eye deformation, cleft palate

Some breed societies brand foals registered with them. This is a painless process although it can look alarming at first! Photo: Chr. Slawik

REGISTERING AND SHOWING YOUR FOAL

More on breed society registration

Before you apply to register your foal with a breed society you need to make sure that its pedigree (its sire and dam) is acceptable under the rules of the stud book concerned, the mating details have been correctly supplied by the stallion owner, and that the covering certificate of the mare and the identification chart and description of the foal have all been correctly completed. Some breed societies also require you to be a member before you register the foal and some (mostly those devoted to one of the pure-bred native breeds) insist on inspecting the foal to check that it conforms to the breed standard before they will register it.

An increasing number of breed societies now require foals to be micro chipped according to new EU regulations and some will also brand foals (usually on the left thigh) upon registration with an emblem specific to that breed.

This brand sometimes includes a 2- or 3-digit number added below for further identification. A complete identity chart, plus written description and all micro chipping and branding details plus details of its verified pedigree are then included in the equine passport issued by the breed society and this document stays with the animal for life.

Equine passports

The equine passport must now accompany a horse or pony whenever it changes keepers, is sold, is sent away for breeding or goes to a competition and it is now illegal to sell a horse if it does not have a passport. It includes your foal's name and registration number (in a standardised 16-digit format known as its Unique Equine Life Number of UELN) as well as details of ownership, date of birth, colour, markings and vaccinations and – in the case of pedigree foals – its verified pedigree. It will also contain a section (known as Section XIV), which you need to complete to indicate if you wish the animal to enter the human food chain upon death. This may seem to be a very distasteful decision to have to make about your young foal but unless you indicate that he or she is not intended for human consumption (by signing the appropriate part of Section XIV) should it fall ill it will not be possible to have it treated with at least 70 % of the medications currently available for horses but banned from the human food chain.

Advice
Check with the breed society about where and when they will be holding foal inspections, micro chipping and branding sessions and plan your diary accordingly. If you miss these dates you might not be able to get your foal registered!

Preparations for a show

You should prepare mare and foal before their first show so that the foal presents itself at its best. Most breeding societies want to see the foal trotting alongside the mare at the end of a long leather lead line attached to a foal head collar, but some – mainly warmblood or sport horse breeding organisations – like to see the foal loose. In either case, it needs to be head collar trained and has to be comfortable with being tied up.

Looking right

It goes without saying that the foal's feet should be properly trimmed, the coat groomed and the mane should be plaited unless it is a native pony in which case its mane and tail should be loose and untrimmed and the feathers on its legs should also be left natural. Different breed societies and showing organisations have different rules for different classes so be sure to check that you are complying with these when you present your mare and foal to the judges.

Correct loading of mare and foal

If your mare is easy to load lead her into the trailer first and let someone push the foal gently in behind her. If the mare does not load well lead the foal onto the trailer first. Be careful to hold it firmly with your hands and arms around it to stop it jumping off again in case the mare does not follow straight away.

There are different opinions about how to travel a mare and foal, but unless the mare and foal are relatively small ponies it is generally

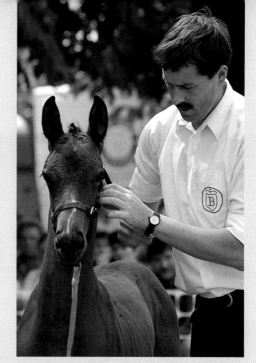

Prepare your mare and foal well to ensure that they show themselves to their best advantage. Photo: Chr. Slawik

best to use one half of a 4-horse box for the pair. However, if you have your own 2-horse trailer this can be used, provided you remove the partition. Pad the front of the trailer with straw bales so that the foal cannot hurt itself in case of you have to brake strongly. A grid should cover the open space between the ramp and the roof.

Never pull the foal along by its head collar. The foal's neck is very delicate and damage to bones, nerves and soft tissue can easily occur. Photo: Chr. Slawik

Horses and ponies that grow up alone or only amongst adult companions, are the most difficult to break in. If you want your youngster to learn proper social skills you have to let it be a horse. Photo: Chr. Slawik

HANDLING THE GROWING FOAL

The importance of companionship

In order to stop your foal becoming a spoiled brat it needs companions of the same age. While playing with its friends, it will develop self-awareness and confidence and therefore good character.

If a foal grows up with only its mother for company or amongst only adult horses it will be either too protected or always the underdog. A horse or pony raised in this way will always be either insecure or rebellious and usually more difficult to handle than one that grew up with companions of the same age.

Mothers always offer protection. Photo: Chr. Slawik

As of day 2 or 3 the foal needs regular exercise in order to burn off energy and develop its lungs, heart and musculoskeletal system properly. Sun and other climatic influences are important for a healthy bone growth (vitamin D metabolism) and a strong immune system.

Foals do not need a rug unless they were born very early in the year or in very bad weather. Of course, there is as much risk in wrapping your youngster up in cotton wool and projecting your need for comfort on to the foal, as there is in the motto: 'if it doesn't kill, it'll cure'. Although adult horses are usually able to control their body heat, foals are less able to do this. You must make sure that the foal does not lie on cold or wet ground especially if it is less than 3 months of age because of the risk of catching a cold or even pneumonia. If the weather is very bad or it is still very cold it is therefore best to restrict the turn out times so that the foal does not get tired while outside and need to lie down to sleep. It is better to turn it out twice a day.

The foal's first teeth

The foal is born with its first teeth already in the mouth. The three molars appear very shortly before birth. The middle incisors emerge after a few days and the next incisors within the first three to eight weeks. The outer incisors appear around the fifth to ninth month.

Worming

Regular worming, at least every eight weeks, is crucial to ensure health and good development of your foal. Make a note of the worming dates in a health plan, as irregular worm-

The foal is born with its first teeth.
Photo: N. Sachs

An open stable with an adjacent paddock is ideal as mare and foal can decide for themselves where to spend the day.
Photo: Chr. Slawik

Advice
If a foal was born very early in the year and gets cold you do not have to buy an expensive rug: an old jumper will keep it warm just as well, although it will not be waterproof if it begins to rain.

This foal is under-developed due to worm infestation.
Photo: Chr. Slawik

The following symptoms can indicate worm infestation:

In the mare
- *Dull coat*
- *Ribs visible despite good feeding*
- *Colic without any obvious cause*

In the foal
- *Generally not looking well (long, matted coat, ribs and hip bones sticking out, malnourished)*
- *Runny eyes and nostrils*
- *Persistent cough that does not improve despite medication*
- *Slow growth*

ing is ineffective. Some worms such as strongyles and roundworms, can cause permanent damage to the lungs and induce allergic, asthma-like reactions, so you should never let it get this far.

Vaccinations

Do not have your foal vaccinated before it is at least 4 months of age as the maternal antibodies in the milk can interfere with the vaccine and render it less effective. Each foal should be vaccinated against tetanus, influenza and herpes. Do not have it vaccinated against everything all at once but have the vaccinations spaced about one week apart (unless you are using combination products). The interval between boosters varies depending on which vaccine is used. Ask your vet when they should be done and make a note of the date in your calendar.

A foal that grows up with only its mother for company cannot become a 'socially competent' horse. Photo: N. Sachs

Providing the essentials

All horses need fresh air, sun and exercise, but foals even more so. If the pregnant mare is kept in a herd with a stable social order you can leave her in the group when giving birth. Otherwise, a separate large foaling box that is bright and airy is ideal. Make sure, however, that there is no draught as foals are very sensitive to it and can catch a cold easily.

Although many studs now use the 'American barn' system of stabling with loose boxes positioned on either side of a central aisle all below an open span roof, wooden stables that face outside provide better climate and airflow and are less prone to problems of circulation and dampness than those constructed from concrete. The humidity in the stable should not be more than 75 per cent. The resting area in the box or open stable should have plenty of dry and high quality straw as the foal will still sleep a lot – up to 9 hours per day. The foal should not be allowed to have a damp coat as the resulting condensation will cool it down and weaken its immune system.

Of course, the foaling box has to be particularly clean as worm larvae can stick to each wet bit of straw that is not removed regularly. Be careful not to injure the foal with the fork when mucking out.

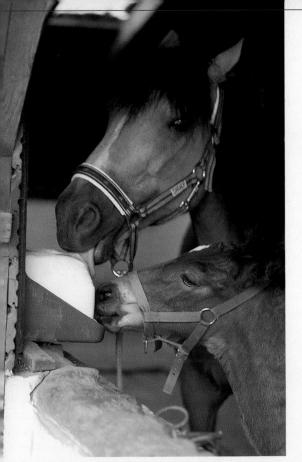

Do not leave a head collar on the mare or her foal when unsupervised. The risk of the foal getting caught up somewhere is too high. Photo: Chr. Slawik

as well. This should all be born in mind when you are designing a paddock for your foal, because muddy or uneven ground or just sand, can lead to the development of bad conformation and hoof problems. Much of the condition of a horse's hoof is a result of its environment. The harder the ground the firmer the hoof will be and vice versa.

Hyperextension (soft pasterns) immediately after birth is a very common occurrence in larger foals (although not normally as extreme as shown here) but is less frequent amongst ponies. The problem usually improves spontaneously through exercise on firm ground. In this case, the foal was perfectly normal after only one week. Photo: K. Kattwinkel

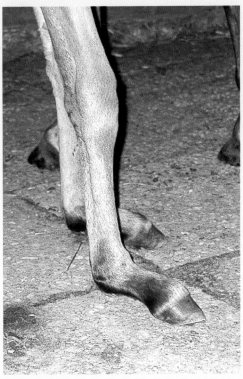

If the box is large enough it is better to put the straw down in the resting area and keep the eating corner clear. Standing on a hard surface is beneficial for the development of hard hooves and good conformation.

The soft pre-natal horn that protects the womb from being cut will wear off quicker on hard ground than soft and tendons, ligaments and bones become stronger on hard ground too. Bad conformation at the time of birth, like a twisted leg or extremely soft connecting tissue that leads to such problems as soft pasterns (hyperextension), often improves spontaneously through walking on firm, even ground

Turn out

Some native pony mares and foals are lucky enough to be turned out in natural herds on large open spaces on mountains, moorlands or woodlands (general described as their 'native heath'). However most breeding animals are now confined to specific paddocks and in this situation a secure field surrounded by a wooden fence at least three rails high or a solid escape-proof hedge is even more important for foals and young horses than it is for adults. Make sure that if you use electric wire it is not so low as to be ineffective but also not so high that the foal can squeeze through or roll underneath. It is important that the whole fence is always live. Foals are curious and can easily get caught in the wire. Every year, many foals need extensive veterinary treatment because of injuries sustained by neglected or unsuitable fencing.

Getting the foal used to being touched is important because the foal's inherited instincts tell it that being touched by another species is an attack. Photo: N. Sachs

With practice, putting on the head collar will soon become routine. Photo: Chr. Slawik

What every foal must learn

Foals need to be taught good manners from the very beginning. This is best done by an experienced person and takes a great deal of time and patience. You therefore need to consider carefully if you can afford this time as doing it by halves will never work. For example, if you live far away from the yard where the foal is and can only see it once or twice a week, you will hardly be able to raise a young horse properly. You can, of course, let other people do this but again, you pay for what you get. Do not leave the foal with amateurs or pseudo-professionals

who are pushed for time. As much as they might like your foal and find it 'sweet', they are often incapable of handling it properly.

Never underestimate the danger that a wrongly brought up young horse can present. Foals have minds like small children but they have the strength of an adult man! They are able to hurt someone seriously.

Get the foal used to the head collar straight away, not just after weaning. Practise this daily as well as touching and picking up its legs and later picking out the hooves. Ask for one exercise at a time but insist on a correct response and then reward the foal immediately. It has to understand three things: nothing bad is going to happen, it has to be obedient and it will be rewarded. If your foal becomes over-confident or tries to bite you, nudge it firmly or push its head away and then treat it completely neutrally again.

Correct leading needs to be practised as well because it is not natural for a horse to walk next to a companion. Wild horses normally walk behind each other and overtaking the horse in front is regarded as a threat.

The foal, therefore, has to learn to walk next to you without fear and must not to be allowed to overtake you. It is best to have a second person available to help. Firstly, place a soft rope around the foal's chest and backside in a figure of eight. If the foal tries to storm off it will feel the pressure against the chest; if it lags behind the pressure comes from the other end. It is important to release the pressure the second the foal gives in!

As soon as this exercise is mastered, you can lead the foal on a head collar and rope next to its mother. Never let leading become a battle

of strength! Do not drag it along if it pulls backwards. The foal might fall over backwards and injure itself.

It is also important that you are able to tie your foal up. When first tying the foal to a wall pull the rope through the hook and just hold it. This helps to prevent injury. Never leave a foal tied up without supervision and always tie the rope to a thin piece of string that breaks easily so that the foal does not hurt itself if it pulls away. Accidents happen quickly and foals can get caught in the rope. Their necks are extremely delicate. Many a foal has damaged itself permanently during tying up manoeuvres that went wrong (e. g. ataxia, paralysis, lameness). Once tied up most foals enjoy a thorough grooming session with humans as much as they do with their equine companions.

Advice
From 12 weeks onwards, you can start to take the foal for a walk without its mother, provided of course that the foal is head collar trained. Do not overdo it though – a few hundred metres away from the stable will be a big achievement. Increase the walks very gradually up to long walks with a young horse until it is old enough to be ridden. The horse will thus develop self-confidence and certainly not cling to other horses.

A foal left alone too early in its life, or for too long periods of time will display signs of distress and panic that can lead to illness or injury. Photo: N. Sachs

Although a foal may appear to be independent when playing with its friends in the field, it is actually still very dependent on its mother for comfort, nutrition and its status in the herd. Any disturbance of this relationship – however temporary – can cause considerable stress to both the mare and her foal. The panic and distress that even short term separation can cause carry with them the risk of not only physical injury, but also illness such as colic or a viral infection and cannot be underestimated.

Most importantly, do not be tempted to ride your mare when she still has her foal at foot. The extra exertion this involves her in could well affect the quality of her milk – and therefore the digestion of the foal. The foal's distress or boredom upon being left on its own in the stable for an extended period makes every corner, wall and piece of equipment a serious safety risk.

Of course, the foal should be accustomed to being left alone for short periods of about 10

Picking up feet is a question of trust. Avoid any form of force.
Photo: D. Schäfer

minutes (so that the mare can be covered again by the stallion for example) but anything more is almost verging on cruelty.

Foot care

Many horse owners do not know that the hoof wall consists of many adjacent horn tubes that grow down from the coronary band continuously. They are surrounded by connecting material. The number of tubes is genetically fixed but the strength and direction of growth can vary. The environment has the greatest influence on these.

It is also true that the stronger the pressure is on one part of the wall, the more vertical the direction of the tubes and therefore hoof growth will become more upright. Horses that live on hard surfaces (e. g. Iberian breeds), usually have steeper and narrower feet than horses on soft ground (e. g. Thoroughbreds). If the ground is predominantly soft and elastic (as in deep litter boxes or field shelters), there is little pressure on the coronary band. The quality and rate of growth of the horn is then not only poor due to the minimised circulation in the coronary band, but the wall also does not grow in a straight line. Flat feet, dropped soles and low heels can be the result.

Ask an expert to evaluate your foal's conformation as early as possible. Photo: Dallmer

Conformational faults can often be corrected relatively easily while the animal is still very young. Photo: Dallmer

This is bad enough for adult horses but in youngsters, problems such as these lead not only to damage of the hooves but also to misalignment of the limbs above as they are still growing and cannot develop correctly above a misshaped hoof.

Many breeders would encounter fewer problems in the feet of these foals if they reduced the deep litter, cleaned the stable more often and let their horses exercise more all year round.

Conformational problems

From the second month at the latest the feet need to be checked and trimmed by a farrier every four weeks. These short intervals are es-

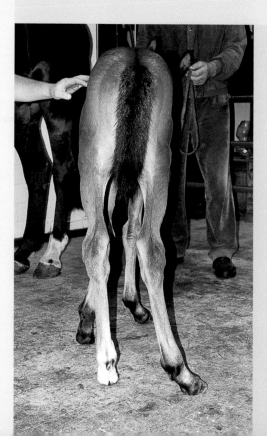

pecially important during this period of maximum growth, as the horn grows as fast the rest of the body.

Misshaped feet may even have to be corrected as often as every two weeks. Do not listen to anyone who tells you otherwise, especially if they say that it will correct itself. Neglected feet have compromised many horses' performance or caused permanent damage.

Hereditary contracted tendons

In this case, the angle of the foot is far too steep due to a shortened flexor tendon and/or weak extensor tendon. Sometimes it may even cause the hoof to be raised off the ground so that it is only touching the ground with its fetlock.

Only mild cases correct themselves spontaneously as the tendons stretch with exercise on hard ground. In many cases, special shoes or support bandages are necessary, but sometimes these only have to be used for a few days. Make sure that bandages are sufficiently padded in order to avoid pressure sores!

This newborn foal has soft pasterns in all four limbs. Even so, plenty of light exercise on hard ground should help to correct it. Photo: Dr. Ende

Club foot

A club foot is also too steep in relation to the pastern axis. This usually only occurs in the front feet.

It can be caused by wear from excessive pawing of the ground or frequent running on hard surfaces. If only one hoof is affected this can be due to mare and foal being kept on pastures with very short grass. Here the foal, whose neck is still short in relation to its height, has to bend one leg backwards to reach the ground. The foal usually bends the same leg all the time.

The constant pressure leads to a shortening of the deep flexor tendon and at the same time, the toe area wears off more while the heels continue to grow. The angle of the foot then becomes steeper. This can develop within a few days. In order to correct this, the heels need to be trimmed at weekly intervals.

Acquired contracted tendons in the yearling

This condition occurs when the bones grow faster than the tendons. It is again important to treat this immediately as once the maximum growth phase is over, permanent problems can remain. A special shoe extending beyond the toe area will force the horse to put more pressure on the heels. This only works on hard ground. The shoe must not sink into the ground, as this will render it useless. If the foal exercises very little by itself it needs to be hand walked on a hard surface twice daily for at least 15 minutes each time.

Unequal leg length

It can sometimes occur that one leg grows faster than the other one. If this does not correct itself quickly the horse will need a 'shoe raise', a special glue-on shoe that will balance out the difference in length. It is necessary to rectify the inequality as soon as possible because the pressure on the growth plates of the bones is higher in the longer leg, so it is better supplied with nutrients and subsequently grows even faster if the inequality increases.

The shoe on the shorter leg raises this leg and thus increases the pressure of the growth plates and stimulates growth.

One hind leg of this colt suddenly became longer than the other one. Photo: K. Kattwinkel

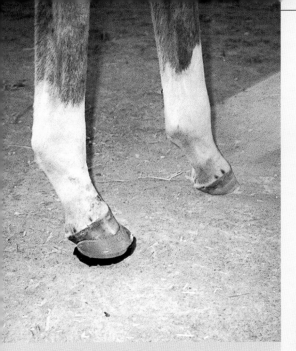

A glue-on shoe on the shorter leg helps to equal the leg length difference. At the same time, the growth plates in this leg are stimulated by the increase in pressure. Photo: K. Kattwinkel

With the shoe in place, the foal's hind legs are equal again. Six weeks later, the legs were of the same length and the shoe could be removed. Photo: K. Kattwinkel

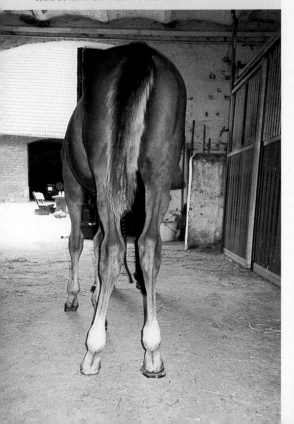

Additional feeding

As a rule, you will not have to feed supplements to your foal during its first three months of life. Foals will start to show interest in hay early. As of week 5, they will already eat a fair amount of other food in addition to milk.

Advice
Many experienced breeders say that foals should not have access to an automatic water drinker before five weeks of age. This is because they could drink too much and have diarrhoea as a result. Others, however, say that this risk is small compared to leaving a foal thirsty should it require more fluid, especially during hot weather.

Obviously, you should only feed a foal with the highest quality food containing all the nutrients necessary to achieve optimal growth, but foals are often overfed with regard to the amount of food as well as nutrient content. The vast choice of supplements, special mixes, treats and powders tempt people into feeding too much. These foals will grow quickly but they often have problems as adults, ranging from metabolic disorders to degenerative joint diseases etc. Fat foals often develop epiphysitis, an inflammation of the growth plates of the long bones that can occur due to excessive pressure on these structures. Extreme loading can also cause these areas to swell up, e. g. in yearlings that gallop a lot on hard ground or during very long journeys. Lack of calcium or imbalanced calcium: phosphorus ratio can also create this condition. If the inflammation is not treated quickly joint problems will be inevitable.

'Couch potatoes' are more prone to develop OCD

Breeders and riders fear these fragments (also called chips or osteochondrosis), particularly in high-performance warmbloods. They develop as a result of disturbances during calcification in the growing joint. The cartilage and bone layers increase in thickness in some places and can no longer be sufficiently supplied by joint fluid. When the cartilage and bone are overloaded they can tear or splinter.

OCD is not a major problem in most pony breeds, but if your foal is a Thoroughbred or a warmblood you can avoid it with correct nutrition and plenty of exercise as the University of Utrecht proved in a study. They divided 43 foals into three groups and fed and kept them under different regimes (stabled with little exercise; stabled with a controlled exercise programme consisting of short intervals of gallop; and thirdly, permanent turn out). The result showed that heavy foals that grew quickly were most prone to joint disease. Reduced exercise increases the risk of joint problems dramatically as does box rest with short intervals of very intense exercise. The foals that are allowed to satisfy their own exercise requirements naturally develop the best.

The youngster knows best how much exercise it requires and will satisfy its needs in the field. Photo: Chr. Slawik

As a foal does not yet produce all of the digestive enzymes it needs, the food has to be easy to eat. Ideally it should therefore have access to grass from a very early age. Grass high in protein is the optimal food for a young horse and on top of that, their requirements for fresh air and exercise can be satisfied at the same time. If you have to feed additional food, use a special trough for foals that has bars across it to prevent the mare's mouth as well as the foal's feet fitting through. It is best to feed a special foal mix formulated for the type of foal you have. These mixes have the advantage that they are based on easily digestive and palatable components and have the correct amount mix of proteins, vitamins and minerals.

Extra portions

The energy requirements of a warmblood or thoroughbred foal are often not satisfied with its dam's milk alone. You then need to feed a commercial foal mix designed for just this purpose. As long as the foal is with its mother, offer the hard feed in a special trough (with bars that only allow the foal to get to it). In an open stable or in the field, you can build a foal shelter. This is an area with a fence of a height that allows only the foal to pass underneath.

If foals are with companions all the time weaning is not quite so bad. Photo: N. Sachs

Non-traumatic weaning

The horse's digestive system is fully independent from eight months of age and it is then ready to be weaned. If a foal is fed additional protein it is possible to safely wean it at 5 to 6 months of age and this is often done in the case of warmblood and sport horse foals. Mentally, however, foals of this age are not mature enough to cope completely without their mother. In nature, weaning happens gradually. Mother and foal chose the right time and usually only when the next foal is due. Even so, you should not let the foal suckle for more than eight months because there is the risk of an overload in nutrients and also indigestion when the adolescent's diet is suddenly changed to hay and straw only. Colics and indigestion can compromise its further development. If you separate foal and mare for a few days, milk production usually ceases. You can then turn them out together again.

Its experiences during weaning and the period immediately afterwards have a strong influence on the foal's further development. An abrupt separation from its mother without contact with familiar companions or a complete change in environment is an enormous psychological stress factor. Various stable vices (more formally known as stereotypical behaviours) can be the result, including weaving, cribbing and napping.

It is better to wean a foal gradually.

Advice
Bach flowers can help minimise the pain of separation:

Beech – when not accepting the unknown (can also help with mares that do not accept their foals at the beginning)

Star of Bethlehem – against trauma

Red Chestnut – against clinging

Walnut – for the new beginning

Honeysuckle – against homesickness

Heather – when foals cling to their mothers

Administer 5–6 drops in 20 ml water/alcohol solution (3:1). Apply this mixture to the forehead every few hours.

How to make weaning stress-free

Raise the foal in a herd where it can build up close relationships with other horses. Together with companions, it will cope with the separation much better.

If keeping it in a herd is not possible, the foal should have at least one companion to live with when it is separated from its mother. Practise short periods of separation from the second or third month onwards.
Leave the foal in its usual friendly surroundings and take the mare to another stable.

Horses as herd animals

All horses are herd animals and enjoy a close family bond. In the wild, a family consists of two or three mares and one stallion and their offspring. Raising the foals is mainly left to the mares.

It is cruel to keep a horse or pony by itself and this is particularly true of a youngster. The foal should be allowed to grow up in a mixed group, not only so that they can play but also because they can learn from their companions. Photo: Chr. Slawik

The more naturally a foal grows up (and ideally in a mixed herd of all ages and sexes), the more normal its behaviour will be later on. Weaning will be easier as well. The foal will also have enough time to find a substitute for its mother when this happens. Groups made up solely of youngsters are like a kindergarten without a nursery teacher. A foal in a herd learns to pay attention to the subtle signals given by other horses. This is important for its social behaviour and will make future training easier. Foals that grow up on their own or

101

amongst only adult horses are often difficult to deal with later on, either because they lack respect for people because they never learned to give in or because they are unwilling to go out alone having always been protected by the older herd members.

Also, the youngsters need play mates of the same age with whom to run around. Only then can muscles and lungs develop properly. A foal living amongst adult horses will exercise a lot less and may even develop vices out of boredom.

When introducing your weanling to a new herd, bear in mind that the other horses might not be particularly friendly towards it. The new member will be bullied and pushed away at first. In order to make life easier for the foal and also to avoid injuries, leave the foal with just one herd member, if possible one of a high rank. Once these two have got used to each other, introduce the others one by one.

When you are looking for somewhere for your weanling to live remember that small studs often offer an adequate environment with individual care for your youngster. Big studs usually have ideal conditions for raising a foal with large fields and open stables but they are often expensive and individual care is hardly possible.

A further option is to take on another foal as a companion. Ideally, make plans for this in the previous year. If you cannot find a foal of the same age, the playmates could be a year older but in either case they should be of equal size in order to avoid playing becoming dangerous for the smaller one.

If you have not got a good field for your foal but want to keep it close by then try and find a private place in your neighbourhood.

Running free in the field is important for the physical as well as mental development of the foal. Photo: N. Sachs

SOME FINAL REMINDERS

The closer we are able to raise our youngsters in conditions that reflect those in which horses lived for the millions of years before we came on the scene, the less likely we are to make mistakes. This applies not only to feeding and management but also to education and training

You can only influence the genetic make up of your foal very slightly, no matter how carefully you select the parents. You are, however, responsible for its further development and therefore for the duration and success of its career as a performance horse. This includes, apart from proper nutrition, plenty of exercise, light, air and sun, and companions, preferably in a herd. None of these basic requirements of the growing horse can be omitted without pay-back.

Wrong nutrition or lack of exercise, for example, will sooner or later lead to health problems and sole confinement to behavioural disturbances.

Continuous slow exercise is the best for a healthy metabolism.

Advice
Do not forget a salt and mineral lick!

Freedom of turn out

If at all possible, young horses should be kept outside. The optimal field consists of 70 per cent of various types of grass, 15 per cent of legumes and 15 per cent of herbs. These plants should be grown slowly in order to allow them to take up plenty of minerals and trace elements from the soil.

Now a few words about pasture hygiene: in order to reduce contamination with worms you will have to clear the droppings off the field at least every other day. If the field is so large that this is not possible do not let the horses overgraze it, which forces them to graze too close to the droppings and eat worm eggs. Regular fertilisation with alkaline fertilisers can help minimise the amount of worms but will not kill all the eggs.

During cold, damp and windy or very hot weather, horses need a shelter which will also help to protect them from insects. Make sure the shelter is sufficiently big or, even better, has partitions or separate entrances, otherwise only the herd leaders will be inside while the others have to stand outside.

You should allow about one week for the change from winter feed to permanent grass. This also applies to the change over in the autumn. You can offer the horse increasing amounts of freshly cut grass while it is still stabled or in a paddock or increase the time of turn out a bit every day starting with an hour per day. It is advisable to feed the horses plenty of hay before turning them out so that they do not overeat on the first bit of grass. Feed hard food at earliest one hour after turn out or hay in order to avoid indigestion.

Important facts about pastures

A pasture offers the ideal basis for nutrition for mare and foal. Pay attention, however, to which fertiliser you use. The saying 'nitrogen weakens the bones' was well known amongst old horse breeders. They needed hardy horses for long agricultural or military use. The mares and foals were kept on large but poor pastures. Yearlings were meant to be skinny. Nowadays, big studs have hardly enough turn out space (some as low as 1 to 1.5 acres per horse). In order to guarantee sufficient grass, many use synthetic nitrogen based fertilisers. Hobby breeders often also do not have the resources, time or the knowledge to manage their fields organically and many farmers do not want to bother. Many metabolic problems (e. g. allergies, damage to the skeleton and early signs of wear) can be traced back to fertilisers. Intensive fertilisation with nitrogen or phosphorus based products block important minerals and trace elements in the soil which then cannot be taken up by the plants and are not available to the horse. The same applies to hay produced on these fields.

Photo: Chr. Slawik

105

The factors that influence growth

Beneficial are:
- Sufficient and high quality food
- Plenty of exercise (increases the appetite, stimulates bone, muscle and ligament development)
- Production of growth hormones is triggered by air, sun and warmth.

Detrimental are:
- Lack of exercise
- Sudden change of food
- Very early weaning (especially when you do not feed enough protein)
- Health problems (e. g. injuries, illnesses, metabolic disorders, parasites)
- Wet and windy climate
- Prolonged cold spells
- Early pregnancy
- Too early or too heavy work
- Psychological stress
- Lack of fun (e. g. a horse in single confinement or a bullied underling)

Allow your horse sufficient time for its physical and mental development! The various pony or horse breeds have very different life expectancies. Therefore, the time to maturity differs as well. Shetland ponies of over 40 years of age are not uncommon whereas a warmblood of 20 years is relatively old and heavy horses rarely reach this age at all. You can roughly distinguish between three groups of maturity:

- Early maturity – heavy horses
- Normal maturity – warmbloods, thoroughbreds
- Late maturity – Arabs, native ponies, Icelandic ponies, Lipizzaners

Many owners and breeders now expect a three year old horse or pony to be fully grown in height and a four year old horse to be able to cope with a full workload. Time is money nowadays! Because of this, many horses not only loose one year of carefree childhood but also 10 years of life expectancy. In mainland Europe the life expectancy of an average warmblood can be as low as 9 years! One forgets that these 'premature' performance horses are not genetically selected for it but solely fed to grow faster. This always compromises constitution and therefore life expectancy.

The modern horse has inherited its genetic make up from its ancestors. In the wild, youngsters are not weaned before the birth of the next foal. The wild horses were as developed at the age of 18 months as modern horses now are at the age of 12 months. The metabolism of horses these days, however, even under optimal circumstances, is only half as efficient as that of their wild ancestors who had to travel up to 100 km per day in order to find food and water. Too much food and excessive weight are therefore always a health risk.

It is far better to raise your foal on a more restricted but balanced diet. It will grow slower than its overfed companions; however, it will still reach its genetically determined size, only a bit later but it will be healthier and

Keeping youngsters in their natural environment is the basis for raising healthy and relaxed horses. Photo: N. Sachs

stronger. Such horses often stay fresh and healthy up to an old age but they will not win shows or competitions as three and four year olds.

The arrival of sexual maturity

When does the foal become sexually mature? This is determined by breed and feeding regime. Well-fed pony and heavy horse fillies can reach sexual maturity as early as in their first autumn. Many pony colts are able to mate at six months. A sudden increase in size of the testicles is a clear indication. Most breeds can be expected to have matured by February of the second year, a little bit later for Arabs and Arab crosses.

Growth rates

The rule of thumb goes: between 30 and 60 days, a foal should have doubled its birth weight.

107

A foal grows most during its first six months. At seven months, it will have reached about 85 per cent of its final height. A warmblood foal, for example, puts on about 800 g per day and weighs about two thirds of its final weight within one year. You can only establish whether your youngster has stopped growing by having x-rays taken of it. The vet can see if the growth plates (physis) of the long bones have closed. Different breeds of horse will have different growth rates. As an example, here is an average growth rate for a warmblood.

Weight increase of a warmblood:

Birth	1.09 m	54 kg
2 months	1.26 m	150 kg
6 months	1.46 m	258 kg
12 months	1.58 m	360 kg
18 months	1.63 m	438 kg
24 months	1.67 m	492 kg
36 months	1.68 m	552 kg

Average growth curve of foals under good, but not intensive conditions

At the end of	weight	height to withers
Birth	9 percent	61–64 percent
2nd month	25 percent	70–74 percent
6th month	43 percent	83–86 percent
12th month	60 percent	91–93 percent
18th month	73 percent	94–96 percent
24th month	82 percent	96–98 percent
36th month	92 percent	97–99 percent

Figures in percentage of the final weight and size of a five to seven year old horse.
(From: Engelmann/Buurmann-Paul "From foal to riding horse")

Advice
If you want to know in advance how tall your foal will become you can use the following rule of thumb: when it is 6 months old, take some string and measure the distance between fetlock and elbow, then the distance between elbow and withers. The foal will grow roughly the difference of these two measurements.

A foal that has a good natural trot should also have one under saddle as well provided it is properly trained and ridden. If a foal has a bad rhythm it will have the same problem as an adult. Photo: N. Sachs

How to recognise the foal's future potential

What a beautiful neck – will it become a dressage horse? Photo: Chr. Slawik

The foal's body will give us a clue what to expect from a future riding horse. The basic conformation, i.e. the angles of forehand and hindquarters, will remain the same throughout its life, as will the rhythm and length of its paces.

The proportions, however, will change. Horses grow more in length than in height. If a foal has a long back it will be even longer when it is an adult. Therefore, the foal's frame should ideally be higher than long. You can then expect it to have good proportions as a riding horse. It is best to evaluate a foal at the age of three days, three weeks or three months and afterwards again at three years.

In the period between three months and three years, young horses often grow in such a way that they loom out of proportion. At one point, they are higher in front, then higher behind. After the third month, they loose their paces because of this imbalance. Therefore, evaluate the length of paces as a foal because it will remain the same all its adult life.

What to look for in a good sport horse foal:

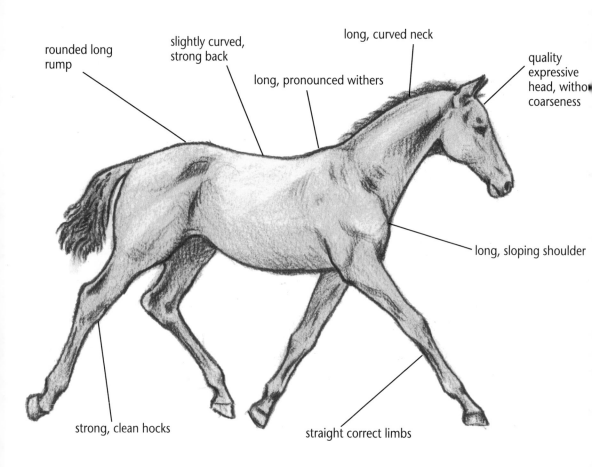

rounded long rump

slightly curved, strong back

long, curved neck

long, pronounced withers

quality expressive head, without coarseness

long, sloping shoulder

strong, clean hocks

straight correct limbs

USEFUL ADDRESSES

Breed societies and stud books

The following organizations maintain lists of approved stallions and will offer advice on how to register your foal with them.

International breeds

Arab Horse Society Windsor House, Ramsbury, Nr Marlborough, Wilts SN8 2PE www.arabhorsesoc-uk.com

General Studbook Weatherbys, Sanders Road, Wellingborough, Northants NN8 4BX www.weatherbys-group.com

Non-Thoroughbred Register Weatherbys, Sanders Road, Wellingborough, Northants NN8 4BX www.weatherbys-group.com

Thoroughbred Breeders' Association Standstead House, The Avenue, Newmaret, Suffolk CB8 9AA www.tbassoc.co.uk

Native pony breeds

British Connemara Pony Society Glen Farm, Waddicombe, Dulverton, Somerset TA22 9RY www.britishconnemara.co.uk

Dales Pony Society Greystones, Glebe Ave, Bakewell, Derbyshire DE45 1TY www.dalespony.org

Dartmoor Pony Society Swn Yr Afon, Thornhill Road, Cwmgwili, LLanelli SA14 6PT www.dartmoorponysociety.com

Eriskay Pony Society Woodcroft, Polinard, Comrie, Perthshire PH6 2HJ marymcgillivray@beeb.net

Exmoor Pony Society Woodmans, Brithern Bottom, Cullompton, Devon EX15 1NB www.exmoorponysociety.org.uk

Fell Pony Society Ion House, Great Asby, Applyby, Cumbria CA16 6HD www.fellponysociety.org

Highland Pony Society Grosvenor House, Shore Road, Perth PH2 8BD www.highlandponysociety.com

New Forest Pony Breeding and Cattle Society The Corner House, Ringwood Road, Bransgore, Hants BH23 8AA www.newforestpony.com

Shetland Pony Stud-Book Society Shetland House, 22 York Place, Perth, Scotland PH2 8EH www.shetlandsponystudbooksociety.co.uk

Welsh Pony and Cob Society 6 Chalybeate Street, Aberystwyth, Ceredigion SY23 1HP www.wpcs.uk.com

Other pony stud books

American Minature Horse Club GB Newclose Farm, Caif Fallow Lane, Norton, Stockton-on-Tees, TS20 1PQ www.mhcgb.co.uk

British Falabella Studbook Burton Farm, Heckington Road, Burton, Swandwine, Sleaford, Lincs NG34 0BX www.thebritishfalabellastudbook.co.uk

British Miniature Horse Society Zeals House, Lower Zeals, Warminster BA12 LG www.bmhs.co.uk

British Show Pony Society 124 Gren Road, Sawtry, Huntingdon, Cambs PE28 5XS www.bsps.com

Caspian Breed Society (UK) Sparrow Farm, Lanhill, Chippenham, Wilts SN14 LX www.caspainbreedsociety.co.uk

Caspian Horse Society Eglentyne, 6 Nun's Walk, Virginia Water, Surrey GU25 RT www.caspianhorsesociety.org.uk

Icelandic Horse Society of Great Britain Oakwood, Curdbridge Lane, Curdridge, Southampton SO32 2BH icehorsestud@hotmail.com

International Miniature Horse and Pony Society Cilmaren House, Caio LLanwrda, Carms SA19 8PN www.imphs.com

National Pony Society Willingdon House, 7 The Windmills, St Mary's Close, Park Street, Alton, Hants GU34 1EN www.nationalponysociety.org.uk

Scottish Icelandic Horse Association Millsburn, Rickarton, StonehavenAB39 3TE www.siha.org.uk

Sports Pony Studbook Society 85 Fishers Field, Buckingham MK18 1SF www.sportpony.org.uk

Warmblood and sport horse breeds

Anglo-European Studbook Ltd PO Box 630 Haywards Heath, West Sussex BN1 2WW www.angloeuropeanstudbook.info

British Bavarian Warmblood Association Sittyton, Straloch, Newmachar, Aberdeen AB21 0RP www.bbwa.co.uk

British Hanoverian Horse Society Ecton Field Plantation, Sywell, Northampton NN8 0BP www.hanoverian-gb.org.uk

British Sports Horse Registry Goblaen House, Rhosgoch, Powys LD2 3JT www.bwbs.co.uk/sport_horse.htm

British Warm-Blood Society Goblaen House, Rhosgoch, Powys LD2 3JT www.bwbs.co.uk

Cleveland Bay Horse Society York Livestock Centre, Murton, York YO1 3UF www.clevelandbay.com

Irish Draught Horse Society (GB) PO Box 1869, Salisbury, Wilts SP3 5XA www.irishdraughthorsesociety.com

Scottish Sports Horse Bickramside Farm, Oakley, Dunfermline, Fife KY12 9LF www.scottishsportshorse.org

Selle Francais / EquiCours 51 Chiltern Drive, Surbiton, Surrey KT5 8LP www.equicourse.com

Sport Horse Breeding of Great Britain 96 High Street, Edenbridge, Kent TN8 5AR www.sporthorsegb.co.uk

Trakehner Breeders Fraternity of Great Britain Bluewood Stud, Lower Lidham, Hill farm, North Lane, Guestling, East Sussex TN36 4IX www.trakehner-breeders.com

Heavy horse breeds

British Percheron Horse Society Three Bears Cottage, Burston Road, Gissing, Diss, Norfolk IP22 5UF www.percheron.org.uk

Clydesdale Horse Society Middleholm Farm, Lesmahagow, Lanarkshire ML11 0HL www.clydesdalehorsesociety.com

Shire Horse Society East of England Showground, Peterborough, Cambs PE2 6XE www.shire-horse.org.uk

Suffolk Horse Society The Market Hill, Woodbridge, Suffolk IP12 4LU www.suffolkhorsesociety.org.uk

Colour-specific breeds

Appaloosa Horse Club (ApHc) UK Ltd Newmans Farm, Newmans Lane, West Moore, Wimborne, Dorset BH22 0LP www.aphcuk.org

British Appaloosa Society Crook Farm, Road Head, Carlisle CA6 6PJ www.appaloosa.org.uk

British Palomino Society Penrhiwllan, LLandysul, Carms SA44 5NZ www.britishpalominoscoiety.co.uk

British Skewbald and Piebald Association Stanley House, Silt Drove, Tippsend, Welney, Wisbech, Cambs PE14 9SL www.bspaonline.com

British Spotted Pony Society Heiffers Farm, Rackenford, Tiverton, Devon EX16 8EW

Coloured Horse and Pony Society (UK) Newton Red House, Mitford, Northumberland NG61 3QE www.chapsuk.com

Spotted Horse and Pony Society Horseshoes, Kelvedon Road, Tolleshunt Darcy, Maldon, Essex CM9 3EL
www.thespottedhorseandponysociety.com

Spotted Pony Breed Society Tollbar Cottage, Coach Road, Butterley Park, Ripley, Derbys DE5 3QW angie@award25.freeserve.co.uk .

UK Paint Horse Association Olde Walnut Tree Farm, Pristowe Green Lane, Tibenham, Norfolk NR16 1PU www.ukpa.co.uk

Other horse breeds

Amercian Quarter Horse Association UK Acresdyke, 63 Laughton Road, Lubenham, Market Horborough, Leics LE15 9TE www.aqha.co.uk

Amercian Saddlebred Association of Great Britain Uplands, Alfriston, East Sussex BN26 5XE www.amerciansaddlebreds,co.uk

British Association for the Purebred Spanish Horse Ltd 21 Rope Walk, Melksham, Wilts SN12 7PW www.bapsh.co.uk

British Morgan Horse Society 7 Redstone, Burghill, Hereford HR4 7RT www.morganhorse.org.uk

British Carmargue Horse Society Valley Farm Riding and Driving Centre, Wickham Market, Woodbridge, Suffolk IP13 0ND www.valleyfarmonline.co.uk

Fjord Horse National Studbook Association of Great Britain Cllyblaidd Manor, Pencarrig, Nr Lampeter, Carms SA40 9QL www.fjord-horse.co.uk

Fjord Horse Registry of Scotland South Denhill, St Katherines, Inveruriem Aberdeenshire, Scotland AB51 0SU www.norwegian-fjord-horse.com

Friesian Horse Association of Great Britain and Ireland Ltd Harbours Hill, Hanbury Road, Stoke Prior, Worcs B60 4AG www.fhagbi.co.uk

Hackney Horse Society Fallowfields, Little London, Haylesbury, Wilts BA12 0ES www.hackney-horse.org.uk

Haflinger Society of Great Britain Wayside Cottage, 2 The Hopground, Finchingfield, Essex CM7 4LU www.haflingersgb.com

Lipizzaner National Studbook Association of Great Britain Cllyblaidd Manor, Pencarrig, Nr Lampeter, Carms SA40 9QL www.lipizzaner.org.uk

Lipizzaner Society of Great Britian Starrock Stud, Ludwell, Shaftesbury, Dorset SP7 0PW www.lipizzaner.co.uk

Lusitano Breed Society of Great Britian Frog Cottage, 20 The Avenue. Camersbach, Cheshire CW9 6HZ www.lusobreedsociety.co.uk

Standard Horse and Trotting Horse Association of Great Britain and Ireland Little Craig, Llandegley, Powys LD1 5UD stagbi@btinternet.com

United Saddlebred Association UK Ltd Merdien House, School Lane, Yardley, Birmingham B33 8PD www.american-saddlebred.co.uk

Emergency help

National Foaling Bank c/o Meretown Stud, Newport, Shropshire, TF10 8BX. Tel: 01952 811234. www.piaffe/org/national_foaling_bank

Feeding and nutritional advice

Baileys Horse Feeds Four Elm Mills, Bardfield Saling, Braitree, Essex CM7 5EJ www.baileyshorsefeeds.co.uk

Dengie Crops Ltd Heybridge Business Centre, 110 The Causeway, Malden, Essex CM9 4ND www.dengie.com

Dodson and Horrell Ltd Kettering Road, Islip, Kettering, Northants NN14 3JW www.dodsonandhorrell.com

Spillers Speciality Feeds Ltd Old Wolverton Road, Old Wolverton, Milton Keynes, Bucks MK12 5PZ www.spillers-feeds.com
NB:There is no national organisation for equine nutrition consultants so it is best to search the internet for one local to you that has knowledge of breeding.

National organizations

British Breeding British Equestrian Federation, National Agricultural Centre, Stoneleigh Park Nr Kenilworth, Warks CV8 2RH www.bef.co.uk/britishbreeding.htm

British Equestrian Federation (BEF) National Agricultural Centre, Stoneleigh Park Nr Kenilworth, Warks CV8 2RH www.bef.co.uk

British Equine Trade Association (BETA) Stokeld Park, Wetherby, West Yorkshire LS22 4AW www.beta-uk.org

British Horse Society (BHS) Stoneleigh Deer Park, Kenilworth, Warks CV8 2XZ www.bhs.org.uk

Central Prefix Register Upper Marshes, Semley, Shaftesbury, Dorset SP7 9AE www.centralprefixregsiter.com

Department for the Environment, Food and Rural Affairs (DEFRA) Nobel House, 17 Smith Square, London SW1P 3JR www.defra.giv.uk/rural/horses/default.htm

National Equine Database (NED On-Line) National Agricultural Centre, Stoneleigh Park Nr Kenilworth, Warks CV8 2RH www.ned.uk.com

Scottish Equestrian Association Grange Cottage, Station Road, Langbank PA14 6 YB www.equinesport.org.uk/sea/web

Scottish Executive Environment and Rural Affairs Department (SEERAD) Pentland House, 47 Robb's Lane, Edinburgh EH14 1TY www.scotland.gov.uk/About/Department/ERAD

Semen agents

Useful sources of information about stallions available by transported fresh, chilled and frozen semen are:

Equine AI Ltd 4 Saddlers Way, Burbage, Wilts SN8 3TY www.equineai.com

Hobgoblins Equine Reproduction Centre Duddleswell, Ashdown Forest, East Sussex TN22 3BH www.hobgoblins-stud.com

International Competition Stallions PO Box 8110, Mauchline, Ayrshire, Scotland KA5 5YB www.internationalcompetitionstallions.com

Stallion AI Services Ltd Twemlowes Hall, Whitchurch, Shropshire SY13 2EZ www.stallionai.com

West Kington Stallion Centre, West Kington Stud, West Kington, Chippenham, Wilts SN14 7JE www.westkingtonstud.co.uk/stallion_centre.htm

World Class Stallions Unit2/3 The Old Barn, Wicklesham, Farringdon, Oxon SN7 7PN www.worldclassstallions.com

Veterinary and related advice

These organizations will help you get in touch with qualified practitioners local to you:

AI Equine Technicians Trade Association Twemlowes Hall, Whitchurch, Shropshire SY13 2EZ www.equineai.org

British Association of Equine Dental Technicians www.equinedentistry.org,uk

British Equine Veterinary Association, Wakefield House, 46 High Street, Sawston, Cambridgeshire CB2 4BG www.beva.org.uk